Private International Law in Argentina

Second Edition

Adriana Dreyzin de Klor

This book was originally published as a monograph in the International Encyclopaedia of Laws/Private International Law.

General Editors: Roger Blanpain, Frank Hendrickx
Volume Editor: Bea Verschraegen

Wolters Kluwer

Published by:
Kluwer Law International B.V.
PO Box 316
2400 AH Alphen aan den Rijn
The Netherlands
Website: www.wklawbusiness.com

Sold and distributed in North, Central and South America by:
Wolters Kluwer Legal & Regulatory U.S.
7201 McKinney Circle
Frederick, MD 21704
United States of America
Email: customer.service@wolterskluwer.com

Sold and distributed in all other countries by:
Turpin Distribution Services Ltd.
Stratton Business Park
Pegasus Drive, Biggleswade
Bedfordshire SG18 8TQ
United Kingdom
Email: kluwerlaw@turpin-distribution.com

ISBN 978-90-411-8268-5

This title is available on www.kluwerlawonline.com

The Author

Adriana Dreyzin de Klor was born in Buenos Aires, Argentina. She earned her doctorate in Law and Social Sciences (*summa cum laude*) at the National University of Córdoba, Argentina. She is the author of 'Mercosur: Generador de una nueva fuente de derecho internacional privado', (Zavalía, Buenos Aires, 1997); 'Los nuevos paradigmas de familia y su influencia en el Derecho internacional', Director, (Advocatus, 2011), El Derecho internacional privado actual, (Zavalía, Buenos Aires, 2015), Los llamados 'Fondos Buitre' en la plataforma internacional (co-author, Rubinzal Culzoni, Santa Fe, 2014), Derecho internacional privado de Costa Rica, (Editora Continental, San Jose, 2014), and many others books in the field of Private International Law (PIL) and Integration Law. She is author/co-author of more than 200 scientific articles in the same fields. She created and co-directed DeCITA (*Revista de Derecho del Comercio Internacional, Temas y Actualidades*) and is director of the Community Law Section of *Revista de Derecho Privado y Comunitario* (Buenos Aires, Rubinzal Culzoni). She is visiting Professor of Postgraduate Studies at Heidelberg Centre (Chile), Universidad Federal de Santa Catarina (Brazil), Universidad de Sao Paulo (Brazil), Universidad Complutense (Spain), Universidad de Castilla La Mancha (Spain), Universidad de Salamanca, Stanford University (USA), UNAM (Mexico), among many others. She has been Juridical Consultant of the Secretariat of Mercosur, Montevideo (2006–2007). She was juridical consultant of ALADI (2007–2008) and European Union Commission (2002–2003; 2005–2006); Juridical Consultant of BID (2005–2006). She is a grantee of the Max Planck Institute of Comparative and International Private Law (Hamburg), and Max Planck Institute of Comparative and International Public Law (Heidelberg). She received Fernand Braudel seniorship at the European University Institute (Italy, 2010). Prof. Adriana Dreyzin is a member of IHLADI (Instituto Hispano Luso Americano de Derecho Internacional); IDEIR (Instituto de Derecho Europeo de Integración Regional); AIDC (Asociacion Internacional de Derecho Comparado). She is academic member of the Mexican Academy of PIL and Comparative Law. Prof. Dreyzin has been arbitrator of MERCOSUR on the Argentine list since 2005*.

* I am deeply thankful to Cristina Britos and Carolina Harrington, since without their kind help, it would have been very difficult for me to write this monograph.

The Author

She is collaborator of the 2014 Civil and Commercial Code Reform Commission as co-author of the Private International Law rules of the 2014 Civil and Commercial Code. Since 2013, she has been Secretary of the Secretariat of Science and Technology at the School of Law and Social Sciences of the National University of Cordoba and has formed part of the Assessment Committee for the admission of researchers to CONICET, Argentina.

Table of Contents

List of Abbreviations

AADI	Asociación Argentina de Derecho Internacional
AC	Argentine Constitution
AHRT	Assisted Human Reproduction Techniques
APMT	Additional Protocol to Montevideo Treaties
Art.	Article
AS	Associate State of MERCOSUR
BO	Boletín Oficial de Argentina
CCC	Civil and Commercial Code
CCL	Commercial Company Law 19,550
CCom.	Commercial Code
CCPLCba.	Civil and Commercial Procedural Law of Cordoba
CIDIP	Conferencias Interamericanas sobre Derecho Internacional Privado
CISG	United Nations Convention on Contracts for International Sale of Goods, 1980
CMG	Common Market Group of MERCOSUR
CNG	Convención Interamericana sobre Normas Generales de Derecho Internacional Privado – CIDIP II Montevideo, 1979
CSC	Convención Interamericana sobre Ley Aplicable a las Sociedades Comerciales – CIDIP II, 1979
CT	Collaborating Team
ED	El Derecho
FNCCL	First National Congress of Civil Law
HRTs	Human Rights Treaties
ICP	International Civil Procedure
IHLADI	Instituto Hispano Luso Americano de Derecho Internacional

List of Abbreviations

IJC	International Juridical Cooperation
IPL	International Procedural Law
JA	Jurisprudencia Argentina
LL	La Ley
MFAITC	Ministry of Foreign Affairs, International Trade and Cult
MJHR	Ministry of Justice and Human Rights
NCivC.	National Civil Court
NCCPC	National Civil and Commercial Procedural Code
OP	Ordre Public
PIL	Private International Law
RC	Reform Commission
RCC	Repealed Civil Code
RDPC	Revista de Derecho Privado y Comunitario
SCJN	Supreme Court of Justice of the Nation
SM	State Member of MERCOSUR
SNCCL	Second National Congress of Civil Law
S.S.N	Superintendencia de Seguros de la Nación
TNCCL	Third National Congress of Civil Law
TMICivL	Treaty of Montevideo on International Civil Law
TMIComL	Treaty of Montevideo on International Commercial Law 1889
TMILComL	Treaty of Montevideo on International and Commercial Law 1940
TMIPL	Treaty of Montevideo on International Procedural Law
TMs	Treaties of Montevideo
UN	United Nations
VCLT	Vienna Convention on the Law of Treaties
WIPO	World Intellectual Property Organization

General Introduction

1. Argentina adopted a federal, republican, and democratic system of government. The Argentine Constitution (AC), adopted in 1853, establishes a tripartite system of government consisting of executive, legislative, and judiciary branches. The first branch is headed by a president. Congress (consisting of senators and representatives) has exclusive power to enact laws concerning federal legislation, including international trade, immigration and citizenship, patents and trademarks.

2. The judicial system is divided into federal and provincial courts. Each system has lower courts, courts of appeal, and Supreme Courts. The supreme judicial power of Argentina is vested in the Supreme Court of Justice of the Nation (SCJN).

3. The AC entitles Congress to enact codes concerning civil, commercial, criminal, and mineral law. In addition, Congress enacts laws on labour and social security. These codes and laws are applicable throughout the country. Provinces enact their own constitutions and procedural codes.

4. The legal system, in general, experienced a significant influence from the European legal tradition and is based on the Continental European system, which finds its origins in Roman law.

5. Judges are bound to rule according to the principles included in codes, statutes, decrees of the executive power, and administrative regulations, but not by decisions of other judges rendered in similar cases. Being not a system of *stare decisis*, rulings of higher courts are not binding upon lower courts. Therefore, court decisions basically provide guidelines for general principles to be applied, making the authority of the precedent only persuasive. Even though judges are not bound to follow precedents, in practice they do so in most cases. In certain situations, if there is no statutory law to follow, courts have developed an important body of case law through numerous precedents applying general principles of law.[1]

1. H. Kritzer (ed.), *Legal Systems of the World. A Political, Social and Cultural Encyclopedia*, vol. I, A-D 64–66 (USA: ABC-Clio, 2002).

6. In 1994, the AC was amended.[2] Chapter I, Part I of the AC, referring to 'Declarations, Rights and Guarantees'[3] was not subject to change. Part II was significantly amended in the area of international law, by establishing the supremacy of international and regional integration law over domestic law. Another important change was made by incorporating Human Rights Treaties (HRTs) with constitutional hierarchy.[4]

§1. Historical Development

7. In 1516, Spaniards discovered Río de la Plata. In 1536, the city of Buenos Aires was founded. Soon thereafter, indigenous population expelled the first settlers, and in 1580, Juan de Garay finally settled Buenos Aires on a permanent basis. The territory of current Argentina remained a Spanish colony until 1816.

8. Napoleon's control over Spain prompted Argentina to declare temporary independence. On 25 May 1810, an assembly meeting at the local council of Buenos Aires (*Cabildo*) overthrew the Spanish government and implemented a provisional governing body. As a result, part of the Spanish legislation was derogated. Some of the previous legal dispositions, notwithstanding, were still applicable, provided they did not contradict new regulations. After several unsuccessful attempts by Spain to regain control, independence was declared in 1816. Provinces refused to be ruled by Buenos Aires; hence, the following decades were marked by civil war between Buenos Aires and the remaining provinces. This period of anarchy ended in 1852, and was followed by the adoption of the AC one year later.

---

2. Law No. 24,309 enacted and promulgated on 29 Dec. 1993 established the need for reform.
3. AC, Arts 1–35.
4. Article 75, inc. 22 establishes:

> The American Declaration of the Rights and Duties of Man; the Universal Declaration of Human Rights; the American Convention on Human Rights; the International Covenant on Economic, Social and Cultural Rights; the International Covenant on Civil and Political Rights and its optional protocol; the Convention on the Prevention and Punishment of the Crime of Genocide; the International Convention on the Elimination of all Forms of Racial Discrimination; the Convention on the Elimination of all Forms of Discrimination against Woman; the Convention against Torture and other Cruel, Inhuman or Degrading Treatment or Punishment; the Convention on the Rights of the Child; in the full force of their provisions, they have constitutional hierarchy, do no repeal any articles of the First Part of this Constitution and are to be understood as complementing the rights and guarantees recognized herein. They shall only be denounced, in such event, by the National Executive Power after the approval of two-thirds of all the members of each House.

It also mentions that 'in order to attain constitutional hierarchy, the other treaties and conventions on human rights shall require the vote of two-thirds of all the members of each House, after their approval by Congress'. Three conventions underwent that procedure and now have constitutional hierarchy: (1) Convention on the Non-Applicability of Statutory Limitations to War Crimes and Crimes against Humanity, (2) Inter-American Convention on the Forced Disappearance of Persons, and (3) Convention on the Rights of Persons with Disabilities and its protocol. The English translations of the AC that are cited throughout this work were extracted from http://www.argentina.gov.ar/argentina/portal/documentos/constitucion_ingles.pdf.

9. Castilian legislation was still in force when the AC was enacted. The AC provided for the enactment of federal codes. In 1862, the entire country adopted what had been the commercial code (CCom.) of the province of Buenos Aires. In 1871, the Repealed Civil Code (RCC) by Dalmacio Velez Sársfield was enacted.

10. Early codes have been subject to many revisions. Amendments can be seen particularly in commercial law, where special legislation has been enacted to deal with the growing complexity of current trade and industrial enterprise. The new legislation has significant impact on Private International Law (PIL).

11. The RCC (Velez Sársfield) was the regulatory body that contained what may be described as the core of domestic PIL. It was enacted in 1869,[5] a time where the object, content, and methodology of the discipline differed significantly from its current prevailing conception. Its once *avant-garde* solutions have been now completely surpassed. An example is found in the connecting factor used to govern the capacity of physical persons, something certainly paradigmatic for that time. Argentina received a high number of immigrants, a fact directly linked to PIL. Consequently, the drafter of the RCC changed the connecting factor of nationality he had adopted in previous drafts and which had been inspired by the Napoleonic Code. The connection given by the principle of domicile adapted best to the reality of a country that welcomed immigration. Notwithstanding, through this choice gains force the territorial tendency that is inbred in the principle of domicile.[6]

12. In 1927, shortly after the enactment of the RCC, the First National Congress of Civil Law (FNCCL) took place in the city of Córdoba. On that occasion, a draft of law reform in the area of PIL was presented, and entitled '*Bases de DerechoInternacionalPrivado para una Ley de Introducción al Código Civil*' (Basic Standards of PIL towards an Introductory Law for the Civil Code) (Basic Standards). That project resulted from the need to cover the changes experienced after the enactment of the RCC. The rationale of these Basic Standards is clearly stated in the Records of the Congress (ActasdelCongreso). The Records state that several amendments were made to the RCC, and, in occasions, they resulted from the pressure exerted by sensitive situations. These pace-meal amendments were defective in purging the weaknesses of the RCC. They also brought dispersion of its rules, and the erosion of its acclaimed harmony and unity.[7]

13. Werner Goldschmidt introduced a unique turn to the methodology of PIL in Argentina during the second half of the twentieth century. That metamorphosis did not affect the existing provisions. Pursuant to ideas adopted in the Second National Congress of Civil Law (SNCCL) of 1937, a structural approach reignited the tendency towards a civil code reform, that this time, would provide legislative

5. Law No. 340, dated 25 Sep. 1869, which made the code effective as from 1 Jan. 1871.
6. J. Samtleben, *Derecho Internacional Privado en América Latina, Teoría y práctica del Código Bustamante.* Vol. I. General Part. Trans. from the original in German C. Bueno-Guzmán (Buenos Aires: Depalma, 1983), 6.
7. *See* Actas del FNCCL, http://www.acaderc.org.ar/biblioteca/biblioteca-virtual/actaprimercongresods civil2.pdf.

autonomy to PIL. The so-called *indirect technique* was adopted from the methodology of PIL, by centralizing the analysis of its problematic on the particular structure of its rules.

14. In 1952, Goldschmidt published the first edition of his '*Bases de unAnteproyecto de Codificación del DerechoInternacionalPrivado*' (Principles for a Draft of a PIL Code). His development responded to the enactment of the AC of 1949,[8] which incorporated changes to fundamental rights and principles, and required a reform to the Argentine system of PIL.

15. Clear notes of normative dispersion and methodological heterogeneity in the system motivated Goldschmidt to work on such a project. In the introduction to his draft, Goldschmidt emphasized two issues: on the one hand, he pointed out the existence of 'intrinsic' defects, and on the other hand, he referred to the defects that 'derived with time'.

16. Amongst the basic problems of domestic PIL is that it does not receive recognition as an autonomous science. Lawyers, notwithstanding, recognize that having an exclusive general part, although marked by normative dispersion, is enough to gain autonomy.[9]

17. The arguments set forth at FNCCL prevailed during the mid-twentieth century. It was considered that even with a 'poor method' the RCC had a set of rules that provided a 'complete system' of PIL.

18. The amendments made between the enactment of the RCC and the publication of the work of Goldschmidt did not produce a change in structure. The idea prevailed that the RCC, as a human construction, was subject to the integration and reform imposed by time and experience. It reaffirmed the importance of overcoming the methodological flaws of the RCC mainly due to the difficulty that its study and mechanism brought, weakening the unity of what was supposed to be a uniform normative body containing all basic rules of Argentine PIL. It made more visible the above-mentioned error: numerous provisions scattered throughout the RCC, containing principles that complement the system and exceed the preliminary title.[10]

19. In 1961, the need to codify the Argentine PIL was reaffirmed during the Third National Congress of Civil Law (TNCCL), held in Córdoba. The idea generated intense debate and found solid resistance. On the one hand, such codification could endanger the integrity of the Civil Law; and on the other hand, Argentine

8. The reform took place during the first government of Juan Domingo Perón. Through this reform, Argentina included in its AC the so-called second-generation rights, which characterize social constitutionalism. The AC of 1949 was abrogated by a proclamation of the de facto military government that resulted from the coup of 16 Sep. 1955.
9. W. Goldschmidt, *Estudios Jusprivatistas Internacionales* (Rosario: UNR, 1969), 140.
10. W. Goldschmidt, 'Reforma del DIPr argentino', *Revista Facultad de Derecho*, Universidad Nacional de Tucumán N° 12, 1955, 169–213.

Congress could have no authority to enact a special law in that area. It was finally recommended that 'experts should work towards systematize PIL within the civil code, as a preliminary title'.[11]

20. In 1968, the RCC was amended by Law Decree 17711/68, yet PIL rules remained unmodified. However, the note passed by the Drafting Committee expressly mentioned the TNCCL recommendation, every time it addressed the need of gathering in a special law the rules of PIL, upon expert opinion.[12]

21. As a reporter to the Seventh Congress of *Instituto Hispano Luso Americano de Derecho Internacional* (IHLADI), Goldschmidt presented an '*exposé de motifs* and basic standards for a uniform law, normative unifying treaty, or model law of PIL'. Years later, in 1973, the Asociación Argentina de Derecho Internacional (AADI) requested from Goldschmidt a new work based on the one developed for IHLADI. The work of Goldschmidt is marked by the division he makes between projects concerning the law applicable to PIL relationships and projects concerning jurisdiction and scope of international procedural law (IPL). Congress did not approve these projects. Codification of PIL was brought again before Congress towards the end of the twentieth century.

22. Regarding codified law and prevailing methodology in the first half of the twentieth century, PIL was conceived as a system of distribution of legislative competences. There, the law and sphere of sovereignty of the authority that passed that law were inseparable. The task of delimiting the respective legislative competences of States (even in private law) belonged to PIL. In this sense, the emerging conflicts derived from the international life of private individuals were moved into the public law sphere. This led to consider the scope of PIL as a set of rules aimed to solve problems of law enforcement using connecting factors as source and remission as technique.[13]

23. However, another respected Argentine doctrinal trend held that the subject matter of PIL is to regulate the interaction of private law relations with foreign elements. This should be characterized by an attitude of understanding and respect towards the existence of human groups or communities living under different legal orders and whose human interactions might be different to those unique to our community. This respect would be reflected in the application of foreign law, since legal relationships may be connected with more than one system or jurisdiction.[14]

11. *See* Acts of the TNCCL, http://www.acaderc.org.ar/biblioteca/biblioteca-virtual/actatercercongresodsciviltomouno2.pdf.
12. *See ED*, t.21, 964.
13. *See* M.S. Najurieta, 'El pluralismo metodológico en el Derecho Internacional Privado actual', *ED*, Buenos Aires, 1064.
14. *See* L. Fermé, *Tratado de Derecho del Trabajo*, ed. A. Vázquez Vialard, T° II, Cap. VII (Buenos Aires: Astrea, 1985), 851.

24. During the late twentieth century, a special commission was appointed to work on a comprehensive reform of the RCC. However, to modify PIL, the Ministry of Justice and Human Rights (MJHR) appointed a subcommittee of experts, which rendered a draft, currently under study by Congress and entitled 'Draft of a Private International Law Code' (Draft).[15]

25. At the same time, court decisions gradually changed the traditional view by assuming mutations of significant consequences. A clear example is the recognition of normative supremacy of international treaties over domestic law, even before the amendments to the AC. Consequently, the SCJN acknowledged, pursuant to Article 27 of the Vienna Convention on the Law of Treaties (VCLT), the supremacy of dispositions contained in international treaties if conflicting with domestic laws. The SCJN was very explicit in this regard, noting that the VCLT gives supremacy to international law over domestic law. It was also stated that an order of hierarchy within the Argentine legal system was encountered. In addition, the SCJN claimed that violation of an international treaty could happen by adopting domestic laws prescribing conducts manifestly contrary to treaties or by the omission of adopting provisions that enable compliance. The supremacy of the treaties, according to the SCJN, is consistent with requirements for international cooperation, harmonization, and integration that Argentina recognizes.[16] The SCJN reaffirmed this legal doctrine in several cases.[17]

26. Accordingly, cases related to PIL, i.e., cases connecting different domestic legal systems are currently solved in Argentina mainly by applying standards contained in the RCC and special laws. Whilst procedural aspects of PIL can be found in the provisions of the National Civil and Commercial Procedural Code (NCCPC), provincial procedural codes, and special laws. The above-mentioned is triggered when an international treaty does not apply.

27. On 23 February 2011, the National Executive Branch issued Decree 191 by means of which the Reform Commission (RC) of the Civil Code made up of Doctors Ricardo Lorenzetti, Elena Highton de Nolasco and Aida Kemelmajer de Carlucci. On 7 October 2014, Law No. 26994, enacted by Congress on 1 October 2014, which sanctioned the new Civil and Commercial Code (CCC) which came into effect on 1 August 2015.

28. The new CCC consists of 2,671 rules and issues relating to PIL appear in the Sixth Book, Title IV (Articles 2594–2671). Incorporating the forenamed title resulted from the need to update the preceding legislation, which was advanced at the time it was created, but today requires reformulation to suit the times we live.

15. Resolution Nº 191/02, modified by Resolution 144/02 of the MJDDHH.
16. *See* cases: SCJN, 22/12/93, *Cafes La Virginia S.A s/ apelación –por denegación de repetición*, *ED*, 158-134, SCJN, 7/7/92, *Ekmedjian, Miguel A. v. Sofovich, Gerarardo y otros*, *LL*, 1992-C, 543.
17. *See* specially, SCJN, 7/7/93, *Fibraca Constructora v. Comisión Técnica de Salto Grande*, *ED* 154-161.

29. The criterion adopted by the RC to draw up the rules for PIL in the CCC consisted in summoning a team made up of specialists to assist in building up the new system. For this purpose, the following doctors in law were called up: Marcelo Iniguez, María Susana Najurieta, María Elsa Uzal and myself, Adriana Dreyzin de Klor.

30. In general terms, and despite not overcoming the plethora of rules which characterized the subject for so long, it is considerably less broken up, where the new PIL regulations constitute significant progress with regard to the former ones. Although the highest aspirations of internationalist private law scholars has not been attained yet relating to the recognition of the legislative autonomy of a scientifically autonomous discipline, the fact that most of the topic has been grouped under a single title, albeit devoted to only two of its three sectors (applicable law and competent jurisdiction), it is a significant step in that direction.

31. The new autonomous PIL acts as an instrument for connecting different legal orders, making use of methodological pluralism in employing rules with differentiated structures (conflict or indirect rules; internationally imperative rules or police rules and material rules, as well as materially oriented rules) and autonomous institutes (e.g., forwarding).[18]

§2. General Principles

32. To establish the principles on which Argentine PIL is build, it is necessary to understand first the country's legal system. Argentina has since 1853 a written AC that is the essential and substantial foundation for the regulatory system and that sets principles in which rules are inspired. Argentine PIL suffers serious complexities due to normative dispersion and successive amendments. However, the order finds grounding in constitutional principles that generate equitable correction of the function of general principles towards valuable decisions. Simultaneously, it develops a change in the system to cover the existing gaps.[19]

33. Constitutionalization of HRTs introduces principles. In many cases, these principles could be detached from the AC; however, they currently comprise a solid core reached through the irrefutable consecration of monism. Increasing importance of monism is closely related to increasing importance of human rights in PIL.

34. Being PIL a component of the State's legal system, and not a watertight compartment, it participates of mutual interdependence and resulting reciprocal

18. *See* A. Dreyzin de Klor, 'A propósito de los principios y las fuentes de las normas de Derecho internacional privado en el nuevo Código Civil y Comercial', *Revista Jurídica de la Facultad de Derecho y Ciencias Sociales*, Vol. II – N° 1 Serie II, www.derecho.unc.edu.ar.

19. *See* A. Boggiano, *Curso de Derecho Internacional Privado. Derecho de las relaciones privadas internacionales,* 5ta. ed. (Buenos Aires: Abeledo Perrot, 2006), 59.

influences, while it spreads under the protection of the AC.[20] Along these lines, it is of particular relevance to PIL the development of essential principles, namely: equality,[21] property,[22] justice,[23] non-discrimination against foreigners,[24]and freedom.[25]

35. Given the normative dispersion that took place throughout time, it was difficult to identify autonomous principles of Argentine PIL. To harmonize legislation with those constant changes, the RCC experienced permanent partial revisions. Hence, Argentina had undergone a constant revision process of the RCC provisions. Legislative enactment had been subject to abuse, understanding that law, as a cultural phenomenon, necessarily responds to historic characteristics, and therefore, evolved together with other Argentine cultural traits.[26] Accordingly, the RCC lost its comprehensiveness because of the large body of laws it included. This phenomenon led to very detrimental effects, of which could be highlighted the impossibility of preserving the general principles that originally comprised the RCC.[27]

36. The situation has changed. Since the new CCC came into effect, there has been a body of laws whose principles emerge clearly from their text. By the same token, it can be claimed that the orienting principles of the new legislation can be identified both in the AC and throughout the articulation and primarily the reading of the Preliminary Note of the new normative corpus.

37. Indeed, one of the characteristics of the new legislation is that Private Law has been constitutionalized. This means that the principles embodied in the AC have been incorporated into the new Code as guiding principles. The axioms that lead the CCC to operate as an instrument for the constitutionalization of Private Law – and PIL as a result – act as guiding principles, following the guidelines laid down by the RC, imbued with a Latin American spirit and feeding on solutions provided by jurisprudence for situations which often lacked normative responses. These gaps can be understood simply by addressing the time when the old Code, a magnificent piece of work by a jurist as wise as Vélez Sarsfield, was created, but it no longer

20. *See* N.P. Sagüés, 'Los tratados internacionales en la reforma constitucional argentina de 1994', *LL*, 1994-E, 1036–1043.
21. AC, Art. 16.
22. AC, Art. 17.
23. AC, Art. 18.
24. AC, Art. 20.
25. AC, Art. 19.
26. *See* R. Lorenzetti. Amongst the claims that support his thesis, and based on showing that 'we are witnessing a progressive re-codification in the area', he notes that 'the Code reflected the creation of a National Government. Its aim was to sort legal conducts of private citizens on an equal basis: a single and equal rule applicable to all citizens, whether nationals or foreigners. (Art. 1, RCC)'. *Las normas fundamentales de derecho privado* (Santa Fe: Rubinzal y Culzoni, 1995), 13.
27. Argentine legal culture is legalistic and formalistic. As a consequence of bureaucracies ever expanding to administer the growing and confusing mass of regulations, the result is exaggerated concern with legal formality. More than 26,000 laws have been enacted so far, but only 3.500 are in force. The abundance of legislation and regulation reflects a mistrust of those administering and interpreting laws. *See* H. Kritzer (ed.), *Legal Systems of the World, A Political, Social and Cultural Encyclopedia*, Vol. I. A-D, 67 (USA: ABC-Clio, 2002).

captures the situations and figures evidenced with the advent of postmodernism. Regulations which pioneered the times and which remained in effect for over a hundred years are no longer suitable to govern the destiny of twenty-first century citizens.

38. The principles on which PIL are built are rooted in the spirit of postmodernism[28] and, specifically, in the adoption of flexible criteria, assuming international jurisdictional cooperation as a duty, in the express incorporation of autonomous will, highlighting the chance to recognize a faculty of the human being and in choosing to include connections answering to links with spatial environments from a logical-axiological perspective, giving the system reasonableness and facilitating the harmonization of solutions.

39. PIL has characteristics that are proper to the normative set that regulates international private legal situations. It is also imbued with the principles[29] upon which it is built; among them, we shall mention the most relevant

- International treaties ratified by Argentina have supremacy over domestic law. If dealing with a HRT, the latter has constitutional supremacy.
- Non-discrimination: contained in Article 20 of the AC, it comes together with the principle of equality. Considered in the field of PIL, it can be understood that Argentina treats all foreign legal systems equally. Nevertheless, if such an application should become incompatible with Argentine public policy, foreign law will not be applicable (CCC Article 2600).
- Principle of equality: all inhabitants are equal before the law, and no distinction is made between them (Article 16, AC). It is clear that the intention of the rule is to prohibit differences between persons based on origin, family, ethnicity, or religion, thus regulating the rights of citizens on the basis of real equality.
- Other constitutional principles above mentioned: Property (Article 17 AC), Justice and Due Process (Article 18 AC), Non-discrimination against Foreigners (Article 20 AC), Freedom (Article 19 AC).
- Principle of 'once capable–always capable': Once persons acquire legal capacity, either in Argentina or while domiciled in another country, they do not lose that status by simply changing their state of domicile (Articles 2616 y 2617 del CCC).
- Principle of protecting the best interests of the child: Cases involving rights of children require special attention to the needs of the child. (Convention on the Rights of the Child). Its application in PIL is invaluable and numerous rulings, mainly in the international return of children, show the scope of this principle, which now has constitutional status in Argentine law.
- Autonomy of parts: before this new unified code came into effect there was no general rule allowing parties to choose the law applicable to their legal relations

---

28. *See* C. Britos, 'Principios del Derecho Internacional Privado en el Proyecto de Código', *La Ley* 13/02/2014, 1,Bs. As., Tomo 2014-A, ISSN 0024-1636.
29. *See*. A. Dreyzin de Klor, *Derecho Internacional Privado actual*, 1° ed., (Buenos Aires: Zavalia, 2015), p. 42.

regarding property, civil and commercial matters. However, it was admitted based on jurisprudence, distinguishing two periods in relation to the interpretation of legislative silence that characterized the previous system. In the first stage, jurisprudence understood that the express lack of a rule implied that autonomy of the parties was not admitted. As from the 1970s, a change took place, resolving that the silence in the code should not be interpreted as prohibiting recognition of the parties' right to autonomy of will. In this sense, the NCCPC expressly stated that it admitted the extension of jurisdiction in personal property-related matters. Article 2651 of the CCC receives the autonomy of will in contractual matters, as we shall see.

- Principle of Justice. In this science, the principle involves respect for the interests existing in external traffic relationships, in which public order tilted in favour of national conceptions should only be considered exceptionally and be conceived as the only path towards international harmony of solutions.
- Due process. This principle, safeguarded by the AC (Article 18) is included in order to illuminate the solution of international private relations, safekeeping procedural axioms such as the equality of all persons before the law, bilateralism and defence during trial, insofar as they are instruments for guaranteeing access to justice for all persons. In the same sense, the obligation to provide jurisdictional cooperation has been incorporated (Article 2611), which must inform international procedural assistance between State authorities (Article 2612).
- The principle of *favor debilis*.This is the assumption provided for in several articles of the international private law scholar sector of the CCC (Articles 2617, 2629, 2630, 2654, 2655, among others), in regulating a relationship subject to several legal orders, prioritizing that which favours the interests of the most vulnerable party in the relationship. In the event of a confrontation between the local legal order and a foreign one, the local order is applied, providing it is more favourable to the validity of the act.

§3. Nature and Scope

40. PIL in Argentina is now an independent legal science. It comprises its own object (i.e., private legal situations with foreign elements) and particular methodology. The indirect method prevails during more than half a century. Currently, it continues in effect with important progress in methodological pluralism. Likewise, the tendency to justice in material law recognizes it place by the influence of international treaties. This is seen, for example, in the United Nations Convention on Contracts for International Sale of Goods (CISG), and UNIDROIT Principles of International Commercial Contracts. The legislation of the NCCC favours the use of these Treaties and Principles from the express recognition of the autonomy of will in contractual matters.

41. A significant development of international jurisdictional cooperation took place in procedural matters. IPL has gained strength, in particular the recognition and enforcement of foreign judgments.

42. The material scope of Argentine PIL comprises:

- Competent jurisdiction in private international legal relations.
- International jurisdictional cooperation in simple or clerical procedural matters, precautionary measure, and recognition and enforcement of foreign judgments.
- Law applicable to legal relations connecting more than one legal system.

§4. Special Characteristics of National PIL

43. Argentine PIL was characterized by the above-mentioned complexities. This was primarily perceived from two interrelated perspectives: substance and methodology. On the one hand, it faced a significant normative dispersion because rules were scattered throughout different normative bodies, such as the RCC, the CCom., the NCCPC, and provincial procedural codes. Special laws related to diverse areas must be added to the above-mentioned texts. These special laws aimed to providing private law remedies. On occasions, they included rules applicable to private law relations with foreign elements. On other occasions, they repealed existing rules, without replacing the rules that originally dealt with foreign traffic. For example, Commercial Companies Law (CCL) (No. 19,550), Bankruptcy Law (No. 24,522), Adoption Law (No. 24,779), Intellectual Property Law (IPL) (No. 11,723, modified by Law 25,036), Law of Name of Natural Persons (No. 18,248), and Law on Immunity of Jurisdiction of Foreign States before Argentine Courts (No. 24,488).

44. This situation makes a full turn with the sanction of the new CCC. On the other hand, the maximum aspiration of international private law scholars is not attained, that which revolves around the recognition of the legislative autonomy of a discipline that is scientifically autonomous. However, the fact that a large part of the subject has been grouped under a single title, albeit devoted to two of its three sectors, is an important step in this direction.

45. Regrettably, important topics are not included in Title IV, Book 6. Thus the section regarding the recognition of foreign decisions that was designed by the Collaborating Team (CT) and raised to the RC was not incorporated into the title. The same thing occurred with the rules relating to companies incorporated abroad. In the first case, the rules contained in the Code of Civil and Commercial Procedure of the Nation and in the provincial procedural orders continue in effect, while regulations concerning companies incorporated abroad continue subject to the provisions of the Commercial Company Law (CCL). Other topics belonging to PIL were not tackled by the team which collaborated with the RC on this matter as we were notified *ab initio* that we were not to include – at this stage at least – regulations for international situations embodied in special laws with autonomous regulations (e.g., PIL regarding sailing, insolvency, insurance and copyright, and related ones). Likewise, the work group we made up did not cover the problem of jurisdictional immunity of States and international organizations.

46. Thus, in PIL, as in law at large, an analysis that seeks to reflect the system cannot limit itself to the study of positive law. It is not possible today to omit practical manifestations because law would be neglected as a social product aimed to reality. Legal formulas, the general precepts required in domestic legislation, should be shown from their judicial application because this science acts as sounding board for transformations in contemporary society.[30]

47. As from the development of this science, by virtue of the increase of multinational private situations in the country and the need to bear in mind the progress of the science over recent decades in a global scenario, external traffic relations have been conditioned by a dynamic unimaginable just a couple of decades ago. Faced with this reality as well as more and more significant operations, there was agreement in that solutions should be designed that were at once simple and relatively flexible, so that the coding could capture situations that appear under factually complex circumstances, high dynamism, and which are often rebellious to rigid classifications.

48. From a general perspective, Argentine PIL is composed of rules of autonomous, conventional, institutional, and transnational dimensions. The first dimension relates to legislation from Congress applicable to particular legal situations with foreign elements that exceed the scope of international treaties. The conventional dimension includes rules developed in international codification forums, and in general, all PIL treaties ratified by Argentina. The institutional dimension refers to PIL rules drafted within the scope of MERCOSUR.[31] The final dimension is *lex mercatoria* or transnational dimension, a typical international source.[32]

49. In most occasions, autonomous rules of PIL are indirect norms; however, there are also material norms. Jointly, they reflect the influence of Friedrich Karl von Savigny, since methodology shows the gravitation of Goldschmidt and the judicial application of much of the last century. Even in the new CCC, this methodology continues to prevail over material, direct methodology, although qualified with regard to the previous legislation. It is still seen in court decisions of the first decade

30. J. González Campos, *Derecho Internacional Privado. Parte especial* (Madrid: Centro de Estudios Superiores, Sociales y Jurídicos Ramón Carande, 1993), 196; C. Britos, 'De cara a la postmodernidad, la superación del conflicto de fuentes a la luz del camino de la coordinación', *Suplemento de Derecho Internacional Privado y de la Integración, El Dial*, 26/11/2010.
31. Argentina, Brazil, Paraguay, Uruguay, and Venezuela share a sub-regional integration, launched by the Treaty of Asunción of 1991. The latter aims to form a common market of the South. PIL rules developed within this process, and they are primarily focused to facilitate international legal cooperation and recognition and enforcement of foreign judgments. The Treaty of Asuncion was followed by, amongst others, protocols on international jurisdiction in contractual matters, international business arbitration, applicable la w in consumer relations, and torts in automobile accidents. *See* M.T. Franca Filho, L. Lixinski & M.B. Olmos Giupponi, *The Law of Mercosur* (Oxford: Hart Publishing, 2010).
32. L. Pereznieto Castro & Silva J., *Derecho Internacional Privado, Parte General,* 10°ed. (México: Oxford, 2015), 165.

of this century, although domestic jurisprudence currently follows a postmodern methodology.[33]

50. Likewise, the international nature of the private situation broadly justifies an autonomous and more flexible regime, on the grounds of the concurrence of exogenous factors, than that which governs internal relations. From this, it can be inferred that the characters of PIL are: (1) statehood, (2) scientific autonomy, (3) exclusivity, and (4) relativism:[34]

(1) The character of statehood lies in recognizing that every country has its own PIL. In Argentina, for example, the rules contained in Book 6 Title IV of the new CCC reflect this character, though not fully as there continues to be certain dispersion in the autonomous PIL as there are several special laws that provide for legal regulation of the matter.
(2) Scientific autonomy poses no discussion whatsoever in Argentina as the country recognizes that it is a differentiated legal discipline. As from the mid-twentieth century, its scientific autonomy has been recognized as it has its own objective, a specific method, and its own system of rules.
The function developed by this science projects into the international domain and captures assumptions of external traffic, unlike civil or commercial law which develop merely within an internal terrain.
(3) The exclusivity of PIL means that when it comes to resolving problems or juridical issues caused by PIL relations, the countries' courts apply their own rules, whatever the dimension, but domestic PIL rules are applied exclusively. In short, this means that Argentine judges apply domestic PIL rules exclusively to: (a) determine the jurisdiction of the courts and authorities of the country in international cases; (b) the law applicable to international private situations, and (c) the legal validity and efficacy in Argentina of judgments delivered abroad. It must be considered that this does not mean that Argentine jurisdictional authorities may not apply foreign law; on the contrary, in numerous assumptions they are duty-bound to do so but it is by virtue of what an autonomous, conventional or institutional Argentine law expresses depending on its origin. That is to say that foreign law is applied based on what is provided for by a federal legislator.
(4) The character of relativism has a double meaning when applied to PIL. On one hand, it means that PIL is different from State to State, an assertion that requires no further explanation as, indeed, Argentine PIL is different from Uruguayan, Venezuelan or any other PIL, as there is no single PIL which is the same for all countries. On the other hand, as every State has its own PIL, the same international private situation is resolved differently or can be resolved in different ways by the authorities of different States since they apply their own system to

33. *See* S. Sanchez Lorenzo, 'Estado democrático, postmodernismo y el Derecho internacional privado'. *Revista de Estudios Jurídicos* N° 10/2010 (España: Segunda Época); A. Dreyzin de Klor, 'La CSJN ubica cada ficha en su casillero', *DeCITA* 11.2009, Insolvencia Internacional, 246.
34. *See* A.L. Calvo Caravaca & J. Carrascosa González, *Derecho internacional Privado*, Volumen I, 14° ed. (Granada: Comares, 2014).

the same case. As a result, relativism in this matter means that the material results of a single case are different from State to State.

As a natural result of the relativism of PIL comes what is often called *forum shopping*, a phenomenon that appears when the parties choose a jurisdiction so that a particular law favouring their expectations becomes applicable. Why can this circumstance be posed? Because private individuals are aware that the same international private situation can be resolved in different ways if it is brought before the court of one State or it is lodged before the courts of another country.

Both the exclusivity and the relativism of PIL bring with them particular consequences. These are adverse results that emerge because each State has its own PIL and its courts apply its PIL exclusively. This situation can encourage a crisis in legal certainty as well as promote surrendering decisions. The latter means that a judgment will beget effects in the country in which it is delivered but will not be recognized in others, because it may not get through the filter represented by frontiers. The existence of surrendering decisions harms the conception of effective legal protection.[35]

The negative effects resulting from the character indicated above can be alleviated by means of legal mechanisms which strengthen the unification of PIL rules in States; this can be achieved by signing international treaties or instruments. Forums for international coding and formulating flexible criteria regarding the validity of extraterritorial judgments are moving in this direction.

35. *See*: P. Mayer & V. Heuzé, *Droit International Privé*, 11e ed. (Francia: LGDJ, Lextenso éditions, 2014).

Part I. General Principles (Choice of Law Technique)

Chapter 1. Sources of PIL

51. Sources are closely linked to the legal nature of law, more precisely, to its origin. From a theoretical perspective, it can be said that a particular legal system contains a variety of rules established according to the principles of the system that generates it. Consequently, to seek the nature of a source is to trace its emergence from the depths of social life into the surface of law.[36]

52. Scholarly writings in Argentina reflect that the term 'sources of law' experiences ambiguity because it is used to designate different facts. Thus, amongst others, the expression is used: (a) to refer to the cause of normative validity, in this sense, the higher rule is source to the immediately inferior rule; (b) as a way of rule creation in which a legislative act is source of rules and rendering a judgment is source of final judgments, customary law, custom, and so forth; (c) as a declaration of rules, in which the AC, laws, and decrees, would be sources of law; and, (d) as the set of patterns consisting of assessments, moral principles, doctrine, and so forth, which determine the intention of the legislature, assisting in providing substance to the rule.[37]

53. In this account, 'sources' are defined as ways of normative manifestation and their ways of expression. These two ways refer to the social forces capable of creating legal rules and the basic categories through which these rules are externalized.[38]

54. Sources must be understood as the required and predetermined forms that external conducts must follow in order to socially receive the protection of the coercive power of law. This concept validates the inclusion of: law, court decisions, custom, Public International Law, and doctrine or legal scholarly writings.

36. F. Martínez Paz, *Introducción al Derecho* (Buenos Aires: Depalma, 1991), 343.
37. M. Osorio, *Diccionario de Ciencias Jurídicas Políticas y Sociales* (Buenos Aires: Heliasta, 1994), 441–442.
38. J. Pérez Royo, *Las fuentes del derecho* (Madrid: Tecnos, 1993), 15.

55. It must be observed that Argentine PIL comprises autonomous rules of PIL, conventional rules, institutional rules, and transnational sources. These dimensions correspond to the areas where rules are created. Hence, when talking of autonomous dimension we refer to domestic law created by national institutions according to their constitutions or domestic regulations. The conventional dimension includes international treaties. The latter dimension includes bilateral and multilateral treaties. The institutional dimension includes treaties of PIL that derive from a process of regional integration. The transnational dimension includes customs and usages and *lex mercatoria*.

56. Autonomous sources of PIL will be addressed first. They apply subsidiarily, that is to say, when a particular situation is out of the scope of a treaty generated by the conventional or institutional dimensions. This claim is currently undisputed because since the constitutional amendment of 1994, international treaties and conventions on integration prevail over domestic law. (see General Introduction §2)

57. The hierarchical order of PIL sources is also supported normatively in Article 2594 of the CCC which expresses verbatim:

> *Legal rules applicable to situations related to several domestic legal orders are determined by the international treaties and conventions in effect applying to the case and, in the absence of rules from a domestic source, rules from an internal source of Argentine private international law are applied.*

58. The sources for this article are the AC, Article 75 subsections 22 and 24; the Vienna Convention on Treaties Law, 1980, Article 27; the Convención Interamericana sobre Normas Generales de Derecho Internacional Privado (CNG), OEA, Montevideo, 1979, Article 1; the Civil Code of Peru, Article 2047 first paragraph, and the General Draft Law of PIL, Uruguay, Article 1.1.

59. Yet the regulations of the AC are rooted in jurisprudence as the modification introduced into the Constitution originates from legal precedents. '*Ekmekdjian c/ Sofovich*' (1992) illustrates this point. Within this line of thought and after the constitutional reform, several court rulings capture the primacy laid down constitutionally, thus consolidating the modification which leads our country to align with a monist internationalist position. As an example, we can cite the case '*Castañeda*' (2007),[39] in which the National Criminal Appeals Court considers the *a quo* court applied correctly the international regulations contained in Article 75 subsection 22 of the AC on domestic law, where the agreement in force in our country prevailed, based on the regulations contained in human rights pacts.

60. To sum up, it is fitting to state that, taking into account the provisions of Article 75 subsections 22 and 24 of the AC, the following hierarchy can be outlined:

39. *See* case: *Castañeda Carlos Antonio s. recurso de casación*, CNCasac. Penal, Sala II, 18/05/2007.

- Those with constitutional hierarchy: Declarations, Conventions, and HRTs according to their force at the time of the constitutional reform. New treaties and conventions on Human Rights require the vote of two-thirds of all members of each Chamber of Congress to achieve equal hierarchy.
- Hierarchically above laws: (a) treaties concluded with States, with international organizations and Concordats with the Holy See; (b) integration treaties that delegate legislative and jurisdictional competence to supranational organisations.

61. We understand that it is not suitable to rank treaties from the conventional dimension equally with those drafted within a process of integration, as such regional schemes are based on principles of mutual trust and operate under other axioms which are proper to them. In addition, upon having provided constitutionally for legislative and jurisdictional faculties to be delegated to supranational organisations, the projection strengthens the relationships between the members of a phenomenon of such characteristics. Granting equal hierarchy to both dimensions poses the possibility of a prospective conflict: consider the existence of treaties from different normative sources (conventional and institutional) ruling on an identical issue and binding the States themselves. Although the incorporation of compatibility clauses – already provided for in the VCLT itself (Article 30) – mitigates the issue, the difficulties do not disappear when the treaties are ranked equally and answer to divergent ends and principles. Let us add that in the same line of thought some of the differences between conventional PIL and institutional PIL that merit the distinction between both dimensions:

The source of production:

The right to integration is generated in the domain of agencies with decision-making authority within MERCOSUR.

Conventional Law is generated in the context of agreements between States or in codification forums.

The subjective domain:

MERCOSUR legal rules are limited to SM and, where appropriate, to AS with regard to their force.

Conventional rules are effective among all the States that ratify them, whether or not they are signatory members they can adhere to such treaties when they are open to the possibility.

The end:

The body of laws of the integration process is compiled with a view to shaping a common market, although today MERCOSUR cannot be considered to be such a thing.

Treaties integrated into the conventional framework mainly seek to facilitate cooperation between countries and the solution of private-legal relationships of external traffic by uniforming sectoral PIL.

62. Acknowledged with a hierarchy lower than that of the Constitution and laws: international agreements entered into by provinces, known by the National Congress, providing they do not clash with State foreign policy or affect the authority delegated to the Federal Government or national public credit.

§1. Domestic Law

63. The CCom. has also been repealed. However, a number of laws containing PIL regulations in their respective areas continue in force. Hence, the Law of Navigation (No. 20,094). The regulations pertaining commercial companies were subject to numerous reforms through special laws which amended the codified provisions; and currently, Law No. 19,550 provides the regulatory framework. The regulations on bankruptcy also lost their original strength by being repealed and replaced with special laws; and bankruptcy is currently governed by Law No. 24,522 which contains rules on PIL.

64. The current rules on international jurisdiction and international judicial assistance are included in the NCCPC and in the provincial procedural codes. For example, the Civil and Commercial Procedural Law of Cordoba (CCPLCba.) provides applicable rules on letter rogatory and recognition, and enforcement of judgments and arbitral awards.[140]

65. The new CCC, aligned with the position that considers that jurisdictional assistance is an indispensable requirement to achieve effective legal protection of the rights of the Parties in an international scenario characterised by legal discontinuity, establishes in Article 2611 that: *'Regardless of the commitments undertaken by international conventions, Argentine judges must provide broad jurisdictional cooperation in civil, commercial and labour matters.'*

66. The source of this rule is to be found in the Protocol of jurisdictional cooperation and assistance in civil, commercial labour, and administrative matters, Las Leñas, Article 1.

67. In those cases in which PIL intervenes, despite the factual unity of the assumption, jurisdictional fragmentation subsists because every State maintains full sovereignty to decide how to act in relation to a particular legal situation within its territory. Faced with the pressing need to encourage States to work together in solving cases in common, the institution of *international jurisdictional cooperation* was developed between nations.

68. The novel incorporation of this rule into the Code is very useful because it provides an essential guideline for Argentine judges to consider international jurisdictional cooperation as a duty, in response to the current world context. Likewise, as it is expressly regulated in the international and conventional framework, though

40. Law 8,465, *BO* 8/06/1995.

as yet without the desired scope, it covers the gap that existed in the autonomous regulation of international jurisdictional cooperation, coordinating different levels of regulation under a single principle.

69. It must be mentioned that, for over a century, the RCC was the body of laws that contained what could well be described as the backbone of domestic PIL. When it was enacted, both the object and the content and methodology of the discipline differed ostensibly from the conception prevailing at present.

70. The new CCC involves significant progress in relation to the new trends and modern conceptions of postmodern PIL. As was expressed in §1 with regard to the historical evolution, PIL rules in the CCC have been compiled in the Sixth Book, Title IV. Although the highest aspirations of internationalist private law scholars has not been attained yet relating to the recognition of the legislative autonomy of a scientifically autonomous discipline, the fact that most of the topic has been grouped under a single title, albeit devoted to only two of its three sectors (applicable law and competent jurisdiction), it is a significant step in that direction.

Unfortunately, relevant topics have been omitted from Title IV, Book 6. Thus the sector regarding the recognition of foreign decisions that was designed by the CT and brought to the RC has not been incorporated into the title. The same occurred to the rules regarding companies incorporated abroad and the regulation of labour contracts in the international domain:

> As for the third sector of the discipline (recognition and enforcement of judgements), the rules contained in the CPCCN and in the provincial procedural systems remain in force, while the regulation of companies incorporated abroad continues subject to the provisions of the Commercial Company Law. Other domains that integrate PIL were not tackled by the CT as we were notified *ab initio* that we were not to include – at this stage at least – regulations for international situations embodied in special laws with autonomous regulations (e.g. private international law regarding sailing, insolvency, insurance and copyright, and related ones). Likewise, the work group we made up did not cover the problem of jurisdictional immunity of States and international organizations.

71. Among the topics that can be considered innovative at the legislative level in the discipline in Argentina are: The structure of Title IV, which is part of the Sixth Book, and consists of three chapters: General Provisions, International Jurisdiction and Special Part.

The first chapter addresses issues that make up the so-called general part of the discipline. The topics included are: application of foreign law, its interpretation and the problems of forwarding, a general clause of exception, internationally imperative rules (of the forum, of applicable law and of foreign States closely linked to the case), fraud against the law, *ordre public (OP)* and a rule for harmonising legal systems.

72. The second chapter entitled '*International Jurisdiction*' contains definitions on attributive jurisdiction criteria and other fundamental institutions. It is the space where the constitutionalization of PIL is clearly seated in that it refers to issues such as access to justice and due procedure, among others, which are essential in international private law cases.

This is a 'sector of a federal nature – as recognized by jurisprudence of the Supreme Court of Justice of the Nation – because it demarcates the domain in which the State itself exercises jurisdictional sovereignty before the jurisdiction of foreign States'. The institutions addressed are: autonomy of will in selecting and extending the jurisdiction, the forum necessitatis, competence for delivering preventive measures, exclusive jurisdictions, the equity forum, regulation of *litispendencia*, jurisdictional cooperation, and international procedural assistance. Also included is a provision about the '*domicile forum or the defendant's habitual place of residence*' and another rule on '*exclusive jurisdiction*', following the general consensus of the doctrine and local jurisprudence.

This chapter closes with the rules relating to '*equal treatment*' and principles of jurisdictional cooperation and international procedural assistance, which place our internal source legislation highly in affinity with the Protocol of Las Leñas regarding cooperation and jurisdictional assistance in civil, commercial, labour, and administrative matters.

73. In Chapter III, Special Part, particular solutions are considered regarding applicable law and the special rules with respect to the attributive jurisdiction criteria in institutions relative to the person, his or her attributes, family relations (marriage, civil unions, kinship, adoption, parental responsibility, and the problem of the protection of children), the disabled; successions, legal entities governed by public law, legal entities governed by public law incorporated abroad, legal acts, contracts in general and consumer contracts, extracontractual liability, security titles, royalties, and prescription.

74. The new PIL acts as an instrument for connecting different legal orders, making use of methodological pluralism in employing rules with differentiated structures (conflict or indirect rules; internationally imperative rules or police rules, among others) and autonomous institutions (e.g., forwarding).

Under the perspective stated above, a particular attitude is imposed upon the judge who must undertake the effort of argumentation. Thus the logic of reasoning is modified with regard to that which is generally developed before their own substantive laws.

The methodology adopted answers to a rigorous criterion for the classification of rules, analysed in the light of the problem posed in this matter by its very nature. The axioms that uphold the construction made and the legal sources that have served as a basis for the new system are rooted in the conception that stems from the constitutionalization of PIL, by receiving the rules and principles that govern the HRTs incorporated into the Constitution in 1994.

§2. Multilateral and Bilateral Treaties

75. Argentina is party to numerous multilateral and bilateral treaties, which are applicable after ratification by an Argentine domestic law. The provisions included in those treaties are considered part of Argentine law.[41]

76. Treaties in force affect Argentine PIL in many ways. On the one hand, it is important to emphasize that international treaties have supremacy over domestic laws. On the other hand, conventions update and modernize domestic PIL. Hence, due to the above-mentioned supremacy, solutions in given cases better suit current times.

77. For example, the CNG of 1979 establishes that foreign law shall be applied by judges and authorities, as done by judges of the State whose law is applicable. Notwithstanding, parties may plead and prove the existence and content of the foreign law invoked. Therefore, CNG advanced significantly over domestic PIL; the latter, on the contrary, considered that to apply foreign law will only be suitable upon request of the interested party. That party must also prove the existence and validity of these laws.[42]

78. Notwithstanding, the role of CNG gains gravitation when reading Article 1:

> Choice of the applicable rule of law governing facts connected with foreign law shall be subject to the provisions of this Convention and other bilateral or multilateral conventions that have been signed or may be signed in the future by the States Parties.
>
> In the absence of an international rule, the States Parties shall apply the conflict rules of their domestic law.

79. Moreover, treaties cover gaps in domestic law. Courts, with the use of analogy, refer to international treaties ratified by Argentina even when these are not applicable to the particular case. An eloquent expression is observed in the decision of the Civil Court of Appeals in the case, *S., B.I. v. C., V. y otro* (CNCiv., Sala I), of 21 November 2002,[43] which states:

> An appeal generally accepted is the application by analogy of the PIL treaties ratified by Argentina. That appeal is accepted even when its direct application does not proceed because the country did not ratify the same treaties as

41. AC, Art. 31: This Constitution, the laws of the Nation enacted by Congress in pursuance thereof, and treaties with foreign powers, are the supreme law of the Nation; and the authorities of each province are bound thereby, notwithstanding any provision to the contrary included in the provincial laws or constitutions, except for the province of Buenos Aires, the treaties ratified after the Pact of 11 Nov. 1859.
42. *See* RCC Art. 13.
43. *ED* 201-154.

Argentina. That appeal is preferred, in principle, over the domestic rules on distribution of territorial jurisdiction.[44]

80. Not considering a treaty enables an appeal before the SCJN, and suffices to qualify a court decision as arbitrary. The SCJN followed this approach in the case *Banco de Italia y Río de la Plata S.A. v. Banco Pan de Azúcar S.A. s/ diligenciapreliminar*, of 9 November 2004:

> This court shares the opinion of the Attorney General. It considers that the Court of Appeals neglected the study of the applicability of international treaties to the case. Hence, this suffices to reject on grounds of arbitrariness the decision appealed before the Supreme Court.[45]

The Attorney General stated there were grounds for arbitrariness:

> since the a-quo [i.e. the tribunal against whose decision has been appealed] avoided the analysis of all issues raised throughout the process. The process dealt with the application and interpretation of Article 35 and related provisions of the Montevideo Treaty on Commercial and International Law of 1940 and of Articles 1, 37, and 56 of the Montevideo Treaty on International Civil Law of 1940.

81. Starting in the late nineteenth century, Argentina actively participates in the development of PIL treaties. Argentina participates, both in the continental and universal level, of global and of partial and progressive codification endeavours. Furthermore, Argentina ratified numerous bilateral agreements.

82. Another essential aspect to be highlighted is its participation as Member State of MERCOSUR. The latter is a process of regional integration comprising Argentina, Brazil, Paraguay, Uruguay, and Venezuela. Conventions of PIL have been ratified within this framework of regional union. Many conventions are enforceable amongst those States and the associated States of Bolivia and Chile.

83. We enumerate below a non-exhaustive list of PIL treaties currently in force in Argentina.

44. It is worth clarifying that in the above-mentioned case, concerning a paternity action, the Court of Appeals considered that even such an analogy did not solve the problem. The Court resolved in that way despite assuming the principle we intend to emphasize: i.e., application by analogy of an international treaty. *See* A. Dreyzin de Klor & D. Fernández Arroyo, *Derecho Internacional Privado argentino. Tratados en vigor y otros textos relevantes* (Buenos Aires: Zavalía, 2009), 10.
45. *LL,* 17/06/2005, 7; *DJ* 26/05/2005, 303.

I. Multilateral Treaties

A. *United Nations*

- Convention on the Recovery Abroad of Maintenance, New York (Law 17,156, *Boletín Oficial de Argentina (BO)* 10/11/67).
- Convention on the Recognition and Enforcement of Foreign Arbitral Awards, New York (Law 23,619, *BO* 4/11/88).
- Convention on Consent to Marriage, Minimum Age for Marriage and Registration of Marriages, New York (Law 18,444, *BO* 24/11/69).
- Convention on the Limitation Period in the International Sales of Goods, New York (Law 22,488, *BO* 02/09/81).
- Convention on Contracts for the International Sale of Goods, Vienna (Law 22,765, *BO* 03/03/83).
- Protocol amending the Convention on the Limitation Period in the International Sale of Goods, Vienna (Law 22,765, *BO* 30/03/83).
- Convention on the Rights of the Child, New York (Law 23,849, *BO* 22/10/90). Currently part of the CN.

B. *Hague Conference on PIL*

- Convention on Civil Procedure (Law 23,502, *BO* 15/10/87).
- Convention Abolishing the Requirement of Legalization for Foreign Public Documents (Law 23,458, *BO* 21/04/87).
- Convention on the Service Abroad of Judicial and Extrajudicial Documents in Civil or Commercial Matters (Law 25,097, *BO* 24/05/99).
- Convention on the Taking of Evidence Abroad in Civil or Commercial Matters (Law 23,480, *BO* 23/04/87).
- Convention on the Law Applicable to Agency (Law 23,964, *BO* 10/09/92).
- Convention on the Civil Aspects of International Child Abduction (Law 23,857, *BO* 31/10/90).

C. *Inter-American Specialized Conference on PIL (Organization of American States)*

- Inter-American Convention on International Commercial Arbitration (Law 24,332, *BO* 17/06/94).
- Inter-American Convention on Conflict of Laws concerning Bills of Exchange Promissory Notes and Invoices (Law 22,961, *BO* 1/11/83).
- Inter-American Convention on Letters Rogatory (Law 23,503, *BO* 16/10/87).
- Inter-American Convention on the Taking of Evidence Abroad (Law 23,481, *BO* 22/04/87).
- Inter-American Convention on the Legal Regime of Powers of Attorney to be used Abroad (Law 22,550, *BO* 15/03/82).

- Inter-American Convention on Conflicts of Laws Concerning Commercial Companies (Law 22,921, *BO* 27/09/83).
- 1979 Inter-American Convention on Execution of Preventive Measures (Law 22,921, *BO* 27/09/83).
- Inter-American Convention on General Rules of PIL (Law 22,921, *BO* 27/09/83).
- Inter-American Convention on Proof of and Information on Foreign Law (Law 23,506, *BO* 20/10/87).
- Inter-American Convention on the Extraterritorial Validity of Foreign Judgments and Arbitral Awards (Law 22,921, *BO* 27/09/83).
- Additional Protocol to the Inter-American Convention on Letters Rogatory (Law 23,506, *BO* 20/10/87).
- Additional Protocol to the Inter-American Convention on the Taking of Evidence Abroad (Law 24,037, *BO* 07/01/92).
- Inter-American convention on support obligations (Law 24,037, *BO* 07/01/92).
- Inter-American Convention on the International Return of Children (Law 24,037, *BO* 07/01/92).
- Inter-American Convention on International Traffic in Minors (Law 25,358, *BO* 26/10/99).

D. Treaties of Montevideo

1888/1889

- Additional Protocol to the Treaties on Private International Law (Law 3,192).
- Treaty on International Civil Law (Law 3,192).
- Treaty on International Commercial Law (Law 3,192).
- Treaty on International Procedural Law (Law 3,192).
- Treaty on International Criminal Law (Law 3,192).
- Treaty on Patent Law (Law 3,192).
- Treaty on Literary and Artistic Works (Law 3,192).
- Treaty on Trademark & Industrial Design (Law 3,192).
- Convention on Free Exercise of Pertinent Activities and Professions (Law 3,192).

1939/1940

- Additional Protocol to the Treaties on Private International Law. Amendments to the Treaty on International Civil Law.
- Treaty on International Commercial Navigation Law (ratified by executive order 7,771/56, *BO* 08/05/1956).
- Amendments to the Treaty on International Civil Law (ratified by executive order 7,771/56, *BO* 08/05/1956).

– Amendments to the Treaty on International Commercial Law (ratified by executive order 7,771/56, *BO* 08/05/1956).
– Amendments to the Treaty on International Procedural Law (ratified by executive order 7,771/56, *BO* 08/05/1956).
– Convention on Free Exercise of Pertinent Activities and Professions (ratified by executive order 7,771/56, *BO* 08/05/1956).
– Treaty on Intellectual Property (ratified by executive order 7,771/56, *BO* 08/05/1956).

II. Bilateral Treaties

A. *Brazil*

– (1990) Treaty for Establishment of Bylaws for Argentine/Brazilian Bi-national Companies (Law 23,935, *BO* 22/05/91).

B. *Chile*

– (1935) Convention on Letters Rogatory (Law 15,989, *BO* 28/11/61).
– Convention Abolishing Consular Legalization Authorizing Minors from Transborder Travel (Law 24,851 *BO* 17/07/07).

C. *China*

– (1990) Agreement to Promote Bi-national Companies (Law 24,096, *BO* 10/07/92).

D. *France*

– (1991) Convention on Judicial Cooperation (Law 24,107, *BO* 04/08/92).

E. *Italy*

– (1987) Convention on Judicial Assistance and the Recognition and the Enforcement of Judgments in Civil Matters (Law 23,720, *BO* 23/10/89).
– (1987) Convention on the Exchange of Certificates on Civil Status and on the Waiver of the Legalization of Documents (Law 23,728, *BO* 23/10/89).

F. Uruguay

- (1980) Convention on Trial Procedures and Letters Rogatory (Law 22,410, *BO* 6/03/81).
- (1980) Convention on the Application of Foreign Law (Ley 22,411, *BO* 06/03/81).
- (1981) Convention on the International Protection of Children (Law 22,546, *BO* 04/03/82).
- (1981) Convention on Legal Cooperation (Law 22,547, *BO* 04/03/82).
- (1991) Convention on Civil Liability on Traffic Accidents (Law 24,106, *BO* 04/08/92).

G. Spain

- (1991) Agreement on the Reciprocal Promotion and Protection of Investments (Law 24,118, *BO* 15/09/92).

H. United States of America

- Agreement on the Reciprocal Promotion and Protection of Investments (Law 24,124, *BO* 25/09/92).

III. MERCOSUR

- MERCOSUR/CMC/DEC. N° 5/92 Protocol on Judicial Cooperation and Assistance in Civil, Commercial, Labour and Administrative Matters (Law 24,578, *BO* 27/11/95).
- MERCOSUR/CMC/DEC. N°5/97 Complementary Agreement to the Protocol on Judicial Cooperation and Assistance in Civil, Commercial, Labour and Administrative Matters (Law 25,222, *BO* 4/01/2000).
- MERCOSUR/CMC/DEC. N° 07/02 Amendment to the Protocol on Judicial Cooperation and Assistance in Civil, Commercial, Labour and Administrative Matters (Law 25,934, *BO* 04/10/2004).
- MERCOSUR/CMC/DEC. N° 11/94 Protocol on the Promotion and Protection of Investment Proceeding from Non-Member Countries of the MERCOSUR (Law 24,554, *BO* 18/10/95).
- MERCOSUR/CMC/DEC. N° 1/94 Protocol of Buenos Aires on International Jurisdiction in Contractual Matters (Law 24,669, *BO* 02/08/1996).
- MERCOSUR/CMC/DEC. N° 27/94 Protocol on Precautionary Measures (Law 24,579, *BO* 27/11/95).
- MERCOSUR/CMC/DEC. N° 1/96 Protocol of San Luis on Civil Liability Resulting from Traffic Accidents between Member States of MERCOSUR (Law 25,407, *BO* 09/04/2001).

– MERCOSUR/CMC/DEC. N° 06/97 Errata to the Protocol on Civil Liability Resulting from Traffic Accidents between Member States of MERCOSUR.
– MERCOSUR/CMC/DEC. Nº 3/98 Agreement on Commercial Arbitration of MERCOSUR (Law 25,223, *BO* 05/01/2000).
– MERCOSUR/CMC/DEC. Nº 4/98 Agreement on International Commercial Arbitration between MERCOSUR and Bolivia and Chile.
– MERCOSUR/CMC/DEC. Nº 13/97 Protocol of Montevideo on Trade in Services of MERCOSUR (Law 25,623, *BO* 15/08/2002).
– MERCOSUR/CMC/DEC. Nº 9/98 Protocol of Montevideo on Trade in Services of MERCOSUR. Sector Annexes to the Montevideo Protocol on Trade in Services of MERCOSUR.

§3. Case Law

84. As stated above, Argentina is a civil law jurisdiction. Jurisprudence is not regarded as a formal source of PIL. In other words, judicial precedents are formally not a source as legal rules. However, jurisprudence is a material source for the interpretation of laws and treaties. Nevertheless, important judgment rendered mainly by the SCJN are carefully studied and generally followed. Judge-made law plays a very relevant role in PIL because statutory law is far from comprehensive.

85. The role of judicial precedents was clearly reflected in the decision in '*Gomez*'. In that case, it was decided that when establishing the application of foreign law there was a 'jurisprudential' acceptance that Treaties ratified by a country are general principles of law according to Article 16 RCC. Therefore, the court applied by its own motion the law of Florida (USA) ignoring the provisions of Article 13 RCC, having as a source the imported case law.[46]

Along the same lines, it has to be emphasized that SCJN rulings are carefully analysed and followed. In the area of PIL, jurisprudence has taken on a very important role as it acts as the source of PIL rules of the new CCC. In addition, legislative-based law is not easy for non-specialist lawyers to understand, and jurisprudence is therefore a very useful ally.

§4. Customary Law

86. The CCC establishes that custom, along with practices and usages, is binding when the laws of the interested parties refer to it, and likewise, it is a source when there are gaps insofar as they do not contradict the law (Article 1).

Custom was recognized in PIL with a particular value essentially in the commercial area through the usage and practices of international trade; the new regulations now establish its character as a legal source with the scope provided for in the text.

Customary rules related to *lex mercatoria* are an important source of law that Argentine courts use when they interpret or apply PIL rules. As an example, in the

46. JNCiv. Nº 29, 01/04/86, *Gómez, Carlos L. s/ sucesión*, *LL* 1987-A-339.

conflict posed by 'Sanovo Internacional SA c/ Ovoprot Internacional', the court used the accustomed application of INCOTERMS to determine the compensation due for non-compliance in the context of an international contract for the sale of goods.

§5. Public International Law

87. International treaties recognizing human rights are particularly important sources of PIL.

88. Furthermore, the VCLT (1969) is of special relevance in the interpretation, application, and validity of sources of PIL.

89. Argentine courts may consider Public International Law, even without formal transposition. For example, court decisions dismissing proceeding against foreign States based on sovereign immunity of defendants.[47] Argentina has specific legislation on this matter.[48] However, the exception does not proceed with the acceptance by the foreign State of Argentine jurisdiction.

§6. Doctrine

90. In Argentina, doctrine or scholarly writings are not a formal source of domestic law. However, it plays a role in PIL because Argentine courts highly regard legal doctrine developed by scholars. Court decisions tend to include references to the academic writings of law professors.

91. Furthermore, in accordance to Article 2 CNG, courts in Argentina shall interpret the applied foreign law subject to the interpretation and practice of the foreign court. Therefore, Argentina shall consider the doctrine that applies in the respective foreign State.

§7. The Interpretation

92. It should be highlighted that in the new CCC interpretation takes on a special character as Article 2 states: '*The law shall be construed taking into account its*

---

47. SCJN, 18/12/07, *Davidoff Constantino v. Reino Unido de la Gran Bretaña e Irlanda del Norte s/ daños y perjuicios*, (Fallos 330:5237). In this case, claims for damages caused by employees of the defendant State – originated in the events of early 1982, which derived in the military actions between Argentina and the UK – against members and property of the corporation. The corporation had lost its infrastructure in Falkland Islands and was banned from continuing with its related commercial activities.
48. Law 24,488, B.O 28/06/1995. This law follows the 'restricted position' of State immunity included in the case *Manauta, Juan J. y otros v. Embajada de la Federación Rusa*, SCJN, 22/12/1994, *LL* 1995-D, 210, with a comment by A. Dreyzin de Klor.

words, its ends, analogous laws, provisions that emerge from treaties on human rights, legal principles and values, in a manner coherent with the legal system in its entirety.'

It is a provision that settles the constitutionalization of Private Law and also PIL which is illuminated by the values and principles inherent to Human Rights, which acknowledge constitutional status.

93. In a similar vein, it is understood that this article is in accordance with SCJN jurisprudence, in that it states that the interpretation must stem from the letter of the law but must be in harmony with it, conforming to the subject matter of the remainder, as its different parts make up a coherent unit and that, in construing its clauses, care is to be taken not to alter the balance of the whole.

94. Pursuant to the guidelines laid down by the AC, it develops under the guiding principles of the HRTs incorporated as from the constitutional reform of 1994, with the huge advantage of recognizing for human beings the individual rights that allow them to exercise their legal standing to make demands at both the domestic and the international level.

Thus, it is that the use of teleological interpretation in PIL assumptions clearly emerges. In this sense, it is determined that the final element is the most important, predicated in every case and not just when the drafting is ambiguous.[49]

49. *See*: Ezquiaga Ganuzas F.J., *La argumentación en la Justicia Constitucional y otros problemas de aplicación e interpretación del Derecho* (Mexico: Tribunal Electoral del Poder Judicial de la Federación, 2006).

Chapter 2. Connection

§1. Choice-of-Law Rules (Conflict-of-Laws Rules)

I. Multilateral/Unilateral Conflict Rules

95. Conflict rules form the basis of Argentine choice-of-law methodology. Most of these rules are multilateral, yet some are unilateral. Multilateral conflict-of-laws rules do not offer a solution per se, but an indication as to which legal order must be applied. Hence, the legal system indicated by the connecting factor (*lex causa*e) can be, in principle, any legal system in the world. Conflict-of-laws rules stipulate the dispositions judges are supposed to apply. This law may be either domestic (i.e., the law of the jurisdiction of the judge) or foreign (i.e., the law of another State).

96. Other conflict-of-laws rules determine when the law of a judge *(lex fori)* is to be applied when facing foreign elements. In other words, Argentine unilateral conflict rules have the same structure as multilateral rules except that they delimit the scope of application of the *lex fori*. Rules of PIL stipulate when to apply the legal system from which they arise. These rules affect areas considered of the utmost importance and are limited to instances where foreign substantive rules rooted in rejected political systems on the issue (*loisd'application immédiate*).[50] Article 10 RCC provided an example in the Argentine system of PIL. Pursuant to this article, immovable located in Argentina were governed exclusively by the RCC. Currently, in accordance with the CCC, the rule is maintained in Article 2667, although it has been drafted in a different tone in indicating in its first part that rights in rem over immovable assets are governed by the law of the place where they are located.

II. Elements of a Conflict Rule

97. The elements of classical multilateral conflict rules reflect the traditional conflict method. These rules comprise:

- a legal category;
- a connecting factor; and
- the applicable law *(lex causae)* as indicated by the connecting factor.

98. It is correct to state that connecting factor and applicable law are the legal consequence of the conflict-of-laws rule. A rule of Argentine PIL helps illustrate this statement.

---

50. G. Kegel, 'Fundamental Approaches', 3 *International Encyclopedia of Comparative Law, Private International Law*, Ch. 3, 13.

99. Article 2644 of the CCC points out the following: 'Succession to the estates of deceased persons is governed by the domicile of the deceased at the moment of his or her death. (…).'

100. The above-mentioned multilateral conflict-of-laws rule provides: (i) a legal category (i.e., law of succession); (ii) a connecting factor (i.e., descendant's domicile); and (iii) an applicable law (*lex causae*) as indicated by the connecting factor (i.e., the law of the domicile the descendent had at the time of death).

III. Legal Consequences

101. According to the principle of equality between *lex fori* and *lex causae*, multilateral rules treat all legal systems equally. Consequently, the multilateral conflict rule aims to pinpoint the most appropriate *lex causae* for a specific matter. It is understood that there is only one appropriate *lex causae,* yet there may be instances where several *lex causae* are available.

102. If no *lex causae* is preferred, the method may play its role. Nevertheless, choice of law involves matters of public policy and order public of the forum. These may refuse to apply an indicated *lex causae* on the basis that such application would contradict its own public policy or public order.

103. OP is understood in the Argentine system as a safeguard for basic moral values and principles of justice of the forum country. The notion of immediately applicable law (policy rule) comprises initially rules designed to guarantee the operation of state administration and state-related activities, and to protect the principle of sovereignty.

104. Unilateral conflict-of-laws rules do not treat all legal systems equally. These rules direct to the sole application of Argentine law. Foreign law may be neglected when interpreting such rules. Article 2667 provides an example of these rules by establishing the application of domestic law when dealing with immovables.

105. According to domestic PIL, now judges apply the foreign law by its own motion. The RCC prescribed another rule. The latter law would be applied only when proof is given and when required by the interested party. Foreign law was considered a fact and not a legal element. Consequently, the court did not strictly apply foreign law. It considered foreign law in the same manner as other factual elements of litigation.[51] Fortunately, this rule changes to the other side according to Article 2595 of the new CCC.[52]

---

51. I. Zajtay, 'The Application of Foreign Law', III *Private International Law, International Encyclopedia of Comparative Law*, Ch. 14, 14-5.
52. A. Dreyzin de Klor, *La aplicación del derecho extranjero. Contratos internacionales. relaciones de consumo*, (Costa Rica: EJC. Serie monografías, 2015), p. 49.

106. The application of foreign law by own motion of the court was accepted by jurisprudence. This was the case even when, as mentioned before, it contradicted the domestic rule[53] and had not been expressly repealed. Story was the source of this rule, who considered foreign law a fact, and therefore, its application derived from the principle of international comity *(comitasgentium)*. 'Comity of nations' expresses best 'the true foundation and extent of the obligation of the laws of one nation within another [and] is the voluntary consent of the latter, and is inadmissible when they are contrary to its known interests'.[54]

107. The evolution of Argentine jurisprudence witnessed the application of foreign law by own motion of the court. There had been certainly cases, although dating to the nineteenth century, in which the SCJN considered that the interested party did not prove foreign law. For example, when dealing with Italian law admitting supplemental prove of the birth of a person (Sent. 24/VII/1894).

108. TMs also consider the law-character of foreign law. The CNG, applying the theory of juridical use presented by W. Goldschmidt, enrols in the theory of the notorious fact which ultimately equalizes foreign law with domestic law.[55] This is the source of the current article of the CCC that regulates the topic by adopting an identical solution (Article 2595).

§2. Connecting Factors

I. Nationality

109. Nationality of individuals is irrelevant under Argentine PIL. It only applies when used as connecting factor in Article 2645. The intention of the codifier, as reflected by the reading of the rule, is to prioritize the validity of a testament. Hence, it reads:

110. A will drawn up abroad is valid in the Argentine Republic pursuant to the forms required by the law of the country where it was drawn up, by the law of the domicile, of the habitual place of residence, or of the testator's citizenship when drawing up the will or by Argentine legal forms.

111. The source of this rule is the article in the former Code. Yet, it is worth mentioning that Velez Sarsfield adopted such principle following initially the position

53. RCC Art. 13: The application of foreign laws, in the cases in which their application is authorized by this Code, can only take place at the request of an interested party who shall have the burden of proving the existence of such laws.

54. J. Story, *Commentaries on The Conflict of Laws, Foreign And Domestic,* 19, 21, 24–25, 37. S. Symeonides, 'United States of America', 3 *Private International Law, International Encyclopedia of Laws* 64, 108–109 (The Hague: Kluwer Law International, 2008).

55. W. Goldschmidt, *Derecho internacional privado, derecho a la tolerancia, 5ta. ed.* (Buenos Aires: Depalma, 1985).

adopted with Eduardo Acevedo when drafting the CCom. of 1862. Velez, notwithstanding, modified his position when drafting the RCC by tending towards domicile, following elaborations provided by F.C. von Savigny.

112. TMs never consider nationality as connecting factor.

II. Domicile

113. Domicile is the most relevant connecting factor in Argentina for matters pertaining to private law.

114. The principle of domicile mainly aims to impose the application of domestic law within the national territory. The intense immigration to Argentina from Europe and other countries, during the period the CCD was drafted, provided a significant sociological factor. The latter helps explain the adoption of domicile.[56]

115. The CCC adopts express definitions. This is new as Vélez's Code failed to provide a clear and precise concept on this point.

Thus in Article 2613 it expresses verbatim:

> Domicile and habitual place of residence of the human person. For purposes of private international law, the human person has:
>
> a) His or her domicile in the State in which he or she resides with the aim of settling there.
> b) His or her habitual place of residence in the State in which he or she lives and establishes lasting bonds.
>
> The human person may not have several domiciles at the same time. In the event that he or she does not have a known domicile, it shall be considered to be his or her habitual place of residence or, failing that, his or her simple residence.

116. We have stated that in PIL the person's legal base is considered to be the link par excellence in determining applicable law and international jurisdiction. Consequently, it is unique for all legal purposes and is identified with the State in which the person settles permanently (domicile) or not (habitual place of residence).

117. Domicile and habitual place of residence do not mean the same in domestic law and in PIL. Whilst in the former it refers to the dwelling where the person lives with the aim of residing there, the latter alludes to the State in which the person's life is centred. Consequently, given that in PIL the domicile – and, alternatively, the habitual place of residence – assumes the status of the person's legal base, it has

56. J. Samtleben, *Rechtspraxis und Rechtskultur in Brasilien und Lateinamerika* (Shaker Verlag: Aachen, 2010), 376.

historically been considered as the connecting point and/or the forum par excellence in determining applicable law and/or the jurisdiction for situations in which no other legal link has been specified.

118. Invoking the domicile and the habitual place of residence as points of connection or forums require both concepts to be qualified, that is to say, their meanings to be accurately specified pursuant to one of the legal systems involved in the legal relationship. In this sense, the Code opts for an autonomous solution, given the fact that rather than referring to a legal order to seek the answer, the rule itself applies a material solution and defines both terms.

119. With regard to the domicile, its configuration requires both factum and animus. In order to obtain a domicile in Argentina, the person must be physically present in the country and must also intend to reside therein for an indefinite time span.[57] For a domicile to be configured, residence must be followed by the intention of remaining in the place permanently, even though the person may be absent momentarily.[58]

120. The habitual place of residence in turn is corpus devoid of animus, that is to say, the place where a person settles for a prolonged period of time, but with no intention of settling there permanently. It is not normally used as a point of connection to determine applicable law because it shows virtually no relationship between the person and the State although this localization is resorted to in some circumstances.

121. Meanwhile, simple residence rarely appears as a localizing contact as in analysing the Law governing the legal situation, a connection with the person is sought, and merely being in a place at a particular moment does not prove such a connection, although this is resorted to in guaranteeing protection in the event of urgent measures being required.

122. PIL does not distinguish between different categories of domicile as can be observed in domestic law. Domestic private law distinguishes between real, legal, and special domiciles. PIL attributes the production of legal effects related to a particular matter to the domicile, and does not therefore admit multiple domiciles. As is accepted peacefully in the doctrine, just as the person is one, so the domicile must be one.

123. If there is no domicile or it is impossible to determine – understood as factum and animus – the law of residence is applied. That is to say, autonomous PIL resorts to the habitual place of residence as the alternative conditional point of

57. S. Feldstein de Cardenas, 'El largo camino recorrido desde Roma al espacio cibernético por el domicilio en el derecho internacional privado', in *El Dial* 25 Feb. 2005.
58. Cam. 1° Apel. Civ., Com., de Paz, Minas, Tributario y Flia. de San Rafael, Mendoza, 'F., *M.C. C/ K., M.s/ Alimentos Provisorios – Compulsa*', 19/08/2015, in http://www.cij.gov.ar/nota-17547-Nuevo-C-digo-Civil-y-Comercial--una-C-mara-fija-alimentos-en-moneda-extranjera.html.

connection (e.g., Articles 2619–2620) irrespective of also admitting the concurrent character of both connections (e.g., Article 2629).

124. Lastly, only when faced with the hypothesis of not being able to establish where the person lives and has durable bonds for a prolonged period of time, should the judge resort to the law of the State where the person has simple residence, that is to say, the place where the person is to be found momentarily, albeit with no permanency.

125. While the RCC was in effect, the domestic PIL system had no chart of categories of its own to define domicile and habitual place of residence, whereby the solution had to be found by resorting to concepts of domestic private law in order to qualify it according to *lex fori*, that is, the law of the court in which the action is brought, in this case the Argentine judge's domestic legal order. The categories of domicile considered therein were legal, special, and of origin.

126. The CCC introduces a relevant modification on this point given the fact that domestic PIL now adopts an autonomous solution to resolve the problem of qualification concerning domicile and habitual place of residence of human persons. To be sure, it is in the legal tradition of the Argentine system to consider the domicile as the centre of gravity, but through the new code it is no longer necessary to build the concept on the basis of elements taken from the domestic legal system.

127. Domicile is a relevant connecting factor in matters concerning, amongst others, civil status; successions (legitimate and testamentary);[59] movable property, concerning the principle of *mobilia sequuntur personam,* in general;[60] and rules relating to personal and proprietary consequences of marriage.[61]

128. According to the TMs (1889 and 1940), domicile constitutes the most important connecting factor. Pursuant to the first treaty, the law of the country of residence will determine the necessary requirements for residence to constitute domicile. Pursuant to the second Treaty, a rule with autonomous qualification establishes the manner domicile will be determined. (1) The habitual residence in a place with the intention to remain in it will be first considered. (2) In the absence of such provision, the habitual residence in the same place of a family group integrated by spouse and minor children or incapable persons will be considered. This will be followed by the criteria of the spouse with whom they are living, or in the absence of the spouse, that of minor children or incapable persons with whom they live. (3) The principal place where spouses perform their business will be then considered. (4) Finally, whenever all the above-mentioned circumstances are not met, domicile will be considered to be that of simple residence.[62]

59. CNCiv., Sala I, 15/08/06, *R.O, L. s/ sucesión, ED* 220-54.

60. CNCom., Sala A, 01/11/07, *Caterpillar Financial Services Corporation v. Guidobono, José M,* C, www. diprargentina.com.

61. Juzg.Fam.Mza., N 4, 04/09/2000, *Kameneva Tatiana p. Sumaria,* Juz.mendoza.gov.ar.

62. TMICivL, Art. 5.

129. Furthermore, the treaties establish that everyone has a domicile, and everyone has only one domicile. There are also rules for determining specific types of domiciles.

III. Habitual Residence

130. As we have seen, habitual residence is a connecting factor in autonomous PIL. It is ruled by a specific provision. In addition, it must be considered that international treaties dealing with choice-of-law rules in force in Argentina often use habitual residence as connecting factor.

IV. Simple Residence

131. Simple residence is used in autonomous PIL. Yet, few rules refer to this connecting factor. First, where the end of Article 2613 expressly states that … *'the human person may not have several domiciles at the same time. In the event that he or she does not have a known domicile, this shall be considered to be his or her habitual place of residence or, failing that, his or her simple residence'.*

V. *Lex Loci Actus*

132. In Argentine autonomous PIL, *lex loci actus* (i.e., law where a transaction took place) is a connecting factor regarding the requirements in areas such as marriages (Article 2622 CCC), and testaments (Article 2645 CCC). Therefore, the place of celebration of a juridical act is a significant connecting factor, mainly when assessing the requirements for its validity (*v.gr.* in writing, before witnesses, or before a public notary).

VI. *Lex Rei Sitae*

133. According to Argentine PIL, *lex rei sitae* applies to conflicts related to immovables. The principle *lex rei sitae* applies to property law matters. That is to say, it applies to acquisition, transfer, and termination of ownership of immovables, and to qualification and legal nature of property located in Argentina (Articles 2663 y 2667).

134. The underlying rationale for the rule is that jurisdiction over immovables vests on the judge of the place of location of the property. According to Argentine law, that is the only court that can render an effective judgment regarding immovables.

135. However, *situs* may be a mere legal fiction. That is the case for certain kind of assets, such as movables with permanent *situs* and registered securities. The legal fiction may be motivated either because the property is not a physical object capable of being located in a particular state or because it is deemed to be situated in the country of registration rather than where it is physically located.[63] Savigny is the source for this doctrine. He stated that every object must be located in some place, and that objects that owners use to carry are different to assets with permanent location (Articles 2669 y 2670, CCC).

VII. Intention of Parties

136. Parties are free to choose the applicable law to their contractual relationship. Nevertheless, the Vélez Code contained no specific rule concerning this issue. The principle gains a place as a usual connecting factor for international contracts by means of jurisprudence.[64] The CCC in Article 2651 provides that parties may choose the law that governs the contract as regards its intrinsic validity, nature, effects, rights, and obligations, for its entirety or for parts thereof Such a choice must be express or may result unequivocally from the terms of the contract and the circumstances of the case. Said possibility is also currently provided for in Article 2605 of the CCC.

137. On jurisdictional grounds, party autonomy related to personal relationship in patrimonial issues is expressly accepted (Article 1 NCCPC). That possibility is also provided by the new Article 2605 CCC.

§3. Changes in Connecting Factors: Change of *Lex Causae*

138. Application of conflict of laws may lead to undesired results. Those results may develop even when all precautions are taken by those formulating a conflict-of-laws rule.

139. Juridical relations, due to their intrinsic nature, are dynamic and tend to shift. Those shifts may occur both in time and in space. Hence, a juridical situation developed in one system may migrate to another system. At the same time, a juridical situation connected with certain systems may migrate those connections to other systems. These are movable conflicts, also referred to as charter change. Therefore,

63. CNCom., Sala A, 01/11/07, *Caterpillar Financial Services Corporation v. Guidobono, José M*, www. diprargentina.com.
64. SCJN, 15/03/1994, *TacticianInt. Corp y otros v. Dirección Gral de Fabricaciones Militares*, *JA* 1994-IV, 67; CNCiv. y Com. Fed., Sala II, 22/07/08, *Zurich Argentina Cia. de seguros S.A. v. Expreso Cantarini S.A. s. faltante y/o avería de carga transporte terrestre*, www.diprargentina.com; Juz. Nac. Com. 16, Secretaría 32, 29/11/04, *Flystone International SA v. Banco Hipotecario SA s/ ejecutivo*, www.diprargentina.com; CNCom., Sala A, 20/03/07, *Raij Kruchik, Abraham v. Banco Hipotecario S.A.*, www.diprargentina.com. *See also*: S. Feldstein de Cárdenas, *Contratos Internacionales. Contracts entered into by computer. Autonomy of will. Lex Mercatoria* (Buenos Aires: Ed. Abeledo Perrot, 1995).

the migration takes place on the element of factual location that underlies the connecting factor of the conflict rule.

140. Juridical consequences of conflict rules may contemplate a change in the *lex causae* that regulates the juridical situations. For example, when the exact moment is established to avoid the new location to cause a time conflict.

141. Argentine PIL provides for a movable conflict in matrimonial agreements and patrimonial relations deriving from marriage. It establishes that rules are subject to the first domicile of the spouses. However, if there is a change in domicile, the law applicable to the relations between spouses will not change, either for property acquired before or after the change in domicile. That is to say, the application of the first domicile of the spouses is preserved. The case of domicile being moved to Argentina is specifically regulated, in which case spouses may opt to apply Argentine Law, so long as it does not affect the rights of third parties and the choice is made by means of a public instrument (Article 2625).

§4. Combination of Connecting Factors

142. A choice-of-law rule generally consists of a set of operative facts matched with a connecting factor. However, on occasions two or more connecting factors may be employed, functioning alternatively, subsidiary, or more rarely, cumulatively. Argentine PIL rarely provides for combinations of connecting factors, though some rare cases may be found. Some rules treat connecting factors as alternatives of equal standing. There are also conflict rules combining connecting factors subsidiary, which means that one is given priority upon others. It is also possible to encounter rules with cumulatively connecting factors.

143. A good example of the alternative point of connection is found in Article 2630 of the CCC, which establishes that:

> *The right to support obligations is governed by the right of the creditor's or the debtor's domicile, whichever the competent authority considers the most favourable in the interests of the maintenance obligation of the creditor.*
>
> *By choice of the Parties, maintenance agreements are governed by the law of the domicile or of the habitual place of residence of either of the parties when entering into the agreement. Failing that, the law governing the right to support obligations is applied.*
>
> *The right to maintenance between spouses or life partners is governed by the law of the last joint domicile, the last effective cohabitation, or the country whose law is applicable to the dissolution or nullity of the bond.*

144. An example of alternative points of connection is provided by Article 2620 in its first part: '*A statement of absence and the presumption of death are governed by the law of the last known domicile of the missing person or, failing that, by the law of his or her last habitual place of residence.'*

145. The rule pertaining to contracts amongst absent parties also provides an example of cumulative connecting factors. An accumulative point of connection is to be found in the last part of Article 2661 of the CCC, which provides: '*If security titles issued in series and publicly offered are involved, the dispossessed bearer shall comply with the provisions of the law corresponding to the issuer's domicile*'.

Chapter 3. Basic Terms

§1. Characterization (Classification)

146. Characterization consists in deciding which conflict rule should be used to determine the legal system that applies to the problem that the judge must resolve. Solutions, two principal and one subsidiary, have been presented because the problem deals with interaction between choice-of-law rules of *forum* and a claim or defence conceived expressly or implicitly in terms of material law of a particular legal system. Qualification could be made by *lex fori,* by *lex causae,* or by an autonomous solution.

147. In Argentina, this problem is referred to as *'calificación'* in English, qualification. Actually, categories of typical institutions are limited in number, but may be expanded. They include status, capacity, marriage, divorce and legal separation, support obligations, guardianship, adoption, corporations, contracts, quasi-contracts, interests on movables and immovables created *inter vivos* or *mortis causa*, formalities, procedure, and foreign judgments.

148. Modern choice-of-law rules focus on broad categories of typical legal institutions. Each category embraces a set of rules of substantive private law.[65]

149. The problem of qualification had not been identified when Vélez drafted the RCC.[66] However, he perceived with notorious intuition the need to determine which law should qualify a relation in which more than one legal system was involved. This intuition of the drafter is perceived in Article 10 RCC, which clearly states that the place of location of the immovable (*lex situs*) will provide the status of the property. It may be inferred that it concerns a *lex fori* qualification because it refers only to immovables locates in Argentina. Notwithstanding, this statement is not definite because the connecting factor directs to Argentine law. Hence, it has been stated that this article produced a qualification both of *lex fori* and *lex causae.*[67] The RCC clearly followed a *lex causae* qualification when dealing with contracts celebrated in one country to be performed in another. This derives from establishing which law rules when determining its nature.[68]

65. *See* K. Lipstein, 'Characterization', 1 *International Encyclopedia of Comparative Law* 4-4. *See also*, A. Menicocci, 'Reflexiones sobre el problema de las calificaciones en el Derecho Internacional Privado', in *El Derecho Privado ante la internacionalidad, la integración y la globalización–Homenaje al Profesor Miguel Angel Ciuro Caldani,* ed. A. Alterini & N.L. Nicolau (Buenos Aires: La Ley, 2005), 617.
66. Kahn and Bartin were the first authors to discuss the problem of qualification (i.e., the case of the widow from Malta of 1897: *Anton v. Bartholo*), followed by Despagnet. *See*, M. Wolf, *Private International Law* 156–144 (2nd ed., Oxford: 1950).
67. *See* Goldschmidt, *Derecho internacional privado*, 90–102.
68. *See* RCC Arts. 1205, 1209, 1210.

150. *Lex fori* qualification means that the terms in Argentina conflict rules are presumed as having the same meaning as their corresponding Argentine domestic law terms. Nevertheless, such a presumption should be disregarded in some cases.

151. In brief, *lex causae* qualification means that the foreign conflict rule designed by the court's law determines the legal system that applies to the pending substantive law problem.

152. Both solutions to the problem of qualification have generated criticism. On the one hand, *lex fori* qualifications provide partial solutions that do not solve the problem because they isolate the law that defines from the law that rules. On the other hand, *lex causae* qualifications generate a vicious circle that generates duplications or gaps in the law. It is impossible to define through *lex causae* if there is uncertainty on which is the *lex causae*.

153. The scope of conflict rules pertaining to the numerous divisions of juridical matters may vary from one legal system to another. Hence, an issue defined as a patrimonial effect of marriage in one country may be deemed to pertain to the law of successions in another. According to Argentine PIL, no methods have been established to delimit whether an issue pertains to a determinate legal category.

154. A first characterization of facts, legal concepts, and categories is necessary in order to find and select the appropriate choice-of-law rule. However, once the choice-of-law rule has designated the applicable law, the problem of characterization returns when identifying the material law of *lex causae* that applies to the subject. Therefore, a second rule of *lex causae* qualification is needed at that stage of the choice-of-law rule application.

155. Within the first fifty years of application of the RCC, courts decided in cases where the problem of qualification arose.[69]

156. Solutions to the problem of qualification could be found in the notes to Vélez Sarsfield's Code. Although the notes are not mandatory sources of law, they acted as guidelines when it came to applying the law. An example of this is provided by the old Article 1211 which invoked the law of the country in which the public instrument was drawn up so that it could be used to define the concept.

157. The new CCC has no notes, but it does have very clear guidelines for its interpretation throughout its Presentation and Preliminary Title, which provide the tools needed to apply it based on the principles of reasonableness and consistency in the search for just solutions.

158. The RC understood that it was convenient not to introduce a regulation for the problem of 'qualifications' because it was preferable to allow the doctrine and

69. CCD 1ª Cap Fed., 8/6/1948, *Maroni Enrique P. v. Mattos Rodriguez Gerardo H.*, *JA* 1948-III, p. 553.

science of PIL to continue its evolution without obliging judges to reason on the basis of abstract criteria. Therefore the doctrinal treatment given to the problem of qualification and the three theses mentioned above to solve it is especially relevant.

159. The RCC in its original drafting did not include autarkic solutions to the problem of qualification. An autarkic classification to the problem consists in using autonomous definitions by which domestic regulations would no longer necessarily determine the applicable substantive law. The PIL system of the new CCC currently incorporates some autonomous qualifications, with the aim of defining some legal categories. Thus it draws on the earlier legislation for some rules, for example, in Article 2623 which states: *'A distance marriage is that for which the absent contracting party expresses his or her consent in person before a competent authority to authorise marriages in the place he or she is in'*, and the last part of Article 2621, which defines the effective conjugal domicile as *'the place where the spouses effectively and indubitably live together'*.

An autonomous solution would be better indicated if the operative facts of the choice-of-law rule were based on an international convention.

160. A case concerning an order of payment provides a better illustration. The order was drafted in Montevideo against a New York bank, and was then endorsed in Argentina by Establecimiento Vitivinícola Sulim Melman S.A. The latter corporation was then taken to court in Argentina. It is hence of interest to determine which law – amongst those related to the international juridical relation – rules on the juridical document. It is worth noticing that the result would have been notoriously different if the document was considered a check or a bill of exchange. The nature of the document would defer if a *lex fori* or a *lex causae* qualification were applied. By applying a *lex causae* qualification, the court determined that it was a bill of exchange (pursuant to Uruguay law, which applied according to Article 23 Treaty of Montevideo on International and Commercial Law (TMILComL) 1940) and decided accordingly.[70]

161. Argentine courts characterize issues before them according to their own legal notions. Therefore, legal institutions unknown to the forum could be another problem when dealing with issues of characterization. In that case, the autonomous system does not offer guidance. Hence, the functional method of comparative law should be applied to select equivalent institutions.

162. The current law on commercial companies includes a provision referring to companies established in foreign jurisdictions pursuant to a structure that is not recognized in Argentine law. That provision states that *lex fori* is applicable, and when dealing with the requirements to be complied for its registration in Argentina,

70. CCivCom. 1ª, Bahía Blanca, 04/10/63, *Establecimiento Vitivinícola Sulim Melman Ltda. S.A., El Derecho*, T. 8, p. 943; *JA* 1964-III, 96. Other precedents that have illustrated the institution of qualifications are: *Tavelli, Augusto Martín s. pedido de quiebra por Espiño, Andrés José*, CNCom., Sala F, 19/05/11;*E. de D., N. R. c. D., M. G. s/ reintegro de hijo*, CNCiv., Sala I, 29/12/04;*Frederick Parker Limited c. Villa, o Villa y Egea*, CNCiv, Sala I, 09/03/90.

it makes them match the highest standards that the law demands to local companies (Article 119 CCL).

163. Corollary, the current jurisprudence does not follow a restricted criterion, and seeks to reach justice in the particular cases. Therefore, the current jurisprudence does not apply a sharp or determinant position. On the contrary, depending on the results, it makes a qualification. This attitude does not imply arbitrariness; it implies the adoption of a methodology in harmony with teleological and axiological criteria that are not bound by the above-mentioned solutions.[71]

§2. Preliminary Question

164. When deciding on a dispute concerning a particular problem, it may be necessary to consider other issues that do not fall within the scope of the conflict of law applicable to the first problem. It may deal with a single legal obligation or liability. It may also deal with a complex legal obligation or liability that is particular to cases of continuous relationship, which determine that one of the conditions predicated by a norm involves a different legal relationship.

165. The existence of a private law relationship may prevent the valid creation of other legal relationships. These are the situations where legal relationships comply with the conditions for a legal effect envisaged by a legal norm. The latter are known as incidental questions or preliminary legal relationships.

166. There are basically two solutions that answer the question generated by the earlier issue. What law shall be applied to regulate it? The theories developed are the theory of equivalence and the theory of hierarchical structure.

167. Through the theory of equivalence, both issues are considered to be on an equal standing; the only difference between them is a question of terminology. No hierarchy is recognized between them, whereby they are to be independently resolved.

It follows from this premise that for the previous issue, the judge consults the PIL rules of the forum determining the domestic law that is applicable. And obviously proceeds thus in relation to the main issue. Consequently, the result is that both aspects of the legal relationship may be regulated by the same or by different laws, according to the indirect rules that govern each assumption.

168. Unlike the one above, the theory of hierarchical structure starts out from the assumption that both issues are related whereby they cannot be resolved independently.

This theory divides into two streams that pose different criteria in finding a solution:

71. *See*: SCJN, 24/02/09, *Compañía General de Negocios pide la quiebra Mihanovich, Ricardo L.*, CNCom., Sala C, 27/04/10, *RDCO* 237, 155/167, with a comment by A. Dreyzin de Klor.

(a) Theory of hierarchical structure under the rule of private law: This theoretical current resolves the main question consulting the PIL of the forum, which determines the law that shall apply. Given how closely it links with the previous issue, the same material law that applies to the main issue corresponds to this one, which is that indicates the point of connection of the indirect rule.
(b) Theory of hierarchical structure under the rule of PIL: This position understands that although there is a link between both issues, it is not as strong a link as considered by the other approach. As a result, the main issue must be resolved consulting the conflict rules of the forum, which determine which law is to be applied. Meanwhile, to resolve the previous issue, the indirect rules of the State whose law is applicable in the main issue must be consulted.

169. The Argentine autonomous PIL system does not contain specific rules on this matter. This question was not considered in Vélez's Code and the criterion followed by the new CCC is not to enclose the topic in an express rule but rather granting the judge freedom and flexibility to resolve pursuant to the corresponding criterion of justice and resorting to the theory of adaptation.

170. As a result of the normative vacuum, court decisions had to solve, starting in 1948, problems generated by the regulation of matters precedent.[72] The inconsistency of results made the matters precedent subject to the law that governed the principal, generating a gentle turn in the jurisprudence.

171. Matter precedent has been addressed in Argentina in cases dealing with successions in which it was necessary to verify the validity of an adoption.[73] Cases dealing with matter precedent also include, amongst others, validity of marriage as a condition to certify a right to inherit and validity of the dissolution of a previous marriage of one of the spouses.[74]

172. The CNG provides that preliminary or incidental issues that may arise from a principal matter 'not necessarily need to be resolved' by the conflict rule on the principal matter.[75]

§3. *Renvoi*

173. This problem relates to interpretation of conflict rules and whether these rules refer to applicable foreign legal systems in their entirety – including its PIL – or only to applicable substantive foreign rules. The latter would mean not to consider the conflict rules of the foreign system, and would not deal with the problem

72. Cam.Civ.2ª CapFed., *Grimaldi, Miguel A. s/ suc*esión, 22/12/1948, *LL* T. 54, p. 513.
73. Juz.Nac.Civ., N° 30, 27/08/73, *Oreiro Miñones, José, s. sucesión,* published in A. Boggiano, *Derecho Internacional Privado, T.I., 5ta. ed.* (Buenos Aires: Abeledo Perrot, 2006).
74. CSJBs.As., *Enrique Bayau s/ suc*esión, *ED* 91-602, and *see* Cam.Nac.Civ., *B., N. s/ sucesión ab-intestato*, CNCiv., Sala I, 29/12/09.
75. *See* Art. 8, CNG.

of *renvoi*. Acceptance or rejection of *renvoi* has not been settled unanimously, but for sure it cannot be admitted or rejected in all cases.[76]

174. In other words, the problem arises because the PIL of one State is different from the PIL of another State. What if the law of one State declares that the law of another State is applicable, but it is then determined that the law of the latter State declares that the law of the first must apply.[77]

175. For *renvoi* to exist, three conditions must be configured: different legal instruments with PIL rules, different points of connection for the same legal situation adopted by each system, and the condition whereby the State of the forum is enrolled in the maximum reference theory, remitting fully to PIL (conflict rules and material rules of domestic law).

176. Until the new CCC was enacted, the subject matter was not provided for by the legal sources binding Argentina in any of their dimensions.[78] In turn, as regards the dominion of case law, there has been no unanimity, historically speaking, with regard to acceptance or rejection, and the attitude of courts has varied depending on the nature of the dispute.

177. However, the new code expressly recognizes the possibility of *renvoi* in Article 2596, which provides that:

> *When a foreign law is applicable to a legal relationship it is also applicable to that country's private international law. If the applicable foreign law forwards to Argentine law, the rules of Argentine domestic law become applicable. When, in a legal relationship, the parties choose the law of a particular country, it is understood that this particular State's domestic law has been chosen, unless it is expressly stated otherwise.*

---

76. L. Pereznieto Castro, *Derecho Internacional Privado*, 234–235.

77. *See*: G. Woodman, *Legal Conflicts and Conflicts of Laws, or it May be True in Theory, but Not Necessarily in Practice*, vol. I, 3 (Bea Verschraegen, *Interdisciplinary Studies of Comparative and Private International Law*, Jan Sramek: Verlag, 2010).

78. The jurisprudence have revealed that;

> Remitiendo el derecho internacional privado argentino al derecho chileno, ha de averiguarse cuál es el derecho que éste considera competente para resolver la cuestión, pues ha de atenderse, en primer lugar, al contenido del derecho internacional privado chileno. Éste carece de norma específica con relación a contratos considerados en general. El art. 16 del Cód. Civil de ese país, cuya aplicación analógica estimo procedente (a otra solución se arriba haciendo aplicación analógica de la regla convencional contenida en el Código Bustamante), se refiere a los bienes sitos en Chile, a los que declara regidos por el derecho del lugar de su situación, sin perjuicio de las estipulaciones contenidas en los contratos otorgados válidamente en país extraño, pero sometiendo los efectos de los contratos a cumplirse en Chile a sus leyes. Debe entenderse que la ley chilena acepta el envío realizado por la ley argentina. (Juz. Nac. Paz 46, 07/10/69, *Estudios Espíndola c. Bollati, Cristóbal J., ED* 33-26).

The sources of this article are Draft Code of International Private Law, Argentina 2003, Article 10, Italian Law of International Private Law, 1995, Article 13; German Introductory Act to the Civil Code, 2009, Article 4 (1), (2).

§4. *Ordre Public* (Public Policy) and Other Exceptions

178. *Ordre public(OP)* is the classical way to exclude the application of foreign law from the process when the foreign law is at odds with the community and the State's fundamental principles and values. That is, it amounts to an exception to the normal operation of the conflict rule by virtue of which the application of the foreign law is discarded, as it does not pass the *test* it is subjected to on the basis of not violating the fundamental principles of the Argentine legal order.

179. The situation of *OP* in Argentina has changed with the reception and constitutional hierarchy of HRTs. Rights and principles included in those treaties are now part of the Argentine juridical system, occupying a paramount position. The incorporation of those treaties with constitutional hierarchy has expanded, as reflected in the practice before the courts, the application of foreign law. Principles that previously were subject to debate or seen as contradicting Argentine legislation are now necessarily applied.[79]

180. The autonomous system of PIL requires a distinction between public policy and *OP*. Public policy is determined by certain local mandatory rules that generally State prohibitions and constitute an absolutely binding minimum standard that undoubtedly applies. In addition, public policy is seen as forming an exception to the application of law, which triggers if an unacceptable result is generated.[80]

181. *OP* plays an exceptional role in preventing the application of foreign law. No definition of *OP* is provided in the Argentine autonomous PIL, not even the doctrine of scholars provides one. Values related to that notion change according to time and place. The content of OP is generally accepted as being determined by the national conception of basic principles underlying constitutional rights and legal norms.

182. This subject matter was received in the RCC through a general clause that indicated non-application of foreign laws when they were at odds with the spirit of the Code's legislation (Article 14 of Vélez Sarsfield's Code). However, the new CCC is expressly recognized in Article 2600, which states: *'Applicable foreign law provisions must be excluded when they lead to solutions that are at odds with the fundamental principles of the ordre public that inspire the Argentine legal order.'*

---

79. Trib.Coleg, Fam., N° 5, Rosario, 24/10/2002, *N. B v. B. G, LL* 2003-D, 351; Juzg.Fam.Mza., N° 4, 04/09/2000, *Kameneva Tatiana p. Sumaria*, juz.mendoza.gov.ar; CNCiv., Sala G, 10/03/2010, *L.L., P.F y otro v. V., R. A*, La Ley online: AR/JUR/3632/2010.

80. *See* P. Lagarde, 'Public Policy', III *International Encyclopedia of Comparative Law, Private International Law*, Ch. 11, 5-3.

183. There are many Argentine court decisions regarding *OP*. Decisions that ban the application of foreign law are mainly rendered in the law of family, divorce, and successions.[81]

184. Decisions on the law of successions are not only motivated by *OP*. Those decisions are mainly intended to avoid the application of foreign law that is considered incompatible with financial matters or immovables.

185. Nevertheless, that exception is applied in Argentine courts only when facing specific and manifest contraventions to essential principles.[82]

186. *OP* hovers between two sectors of PIL, namely: applicable law and the recognition of sentences, although its scope as an exception has been tempered as the incorporation of constitutionally ranking HRTs favour a universal conception of OP which is highly beneficial to protagonists in family law from the axiological view impregnated by the subject matter.

On the other hand, intervention of the *OP* clause is less intense in those sectors in which there are few basic regulating principles, and autonomy of will can develop within a broad field of action. (i.e., to say, in contractual matters, those of public liability, etc.)

187. The additional protocols to the TMs 1889/1940 establish a specific rule that defines the exception of *OP*. The rule states that the law of other States shall never apply against political institutions, laws of OP, or principles of morality of the place of origin.[83]

188. The CNG also provides a rule for *OP* in Article 5: 'law declared applicable by a convention on PIL may be denied application in the territory of a State Party that considers it manifestly contrary to the principles of its public policy (*ordre public*).'

189. It is appropriate to say that CNG does not limit the exception of public policy to cases where application of foreign law contradicts public policy. Courts when deciding can consider whether the law manifestly contradicts the principles of public policy.[84]

---

81. CNCiv., Sala D, 29/02/2008, *Szmuleweiz Segismundo s/ información sumaria*, www.diprargentina.com; Juz. Civ. y Com., Pergamino, 02/02/2009, *C., A. M. v. R., O.J.*, www.diprargentina.com.
82. SCJN, 14/09/10, *Boo, Héctor José s. sucesión testamentaria*, www.diprargentina.com. Recently, case law has addressed the subject of ordre public in the following cases: CNCiv., Sala I, 29/12/09, *B., N. s. sucesiónab intestato*; SCJN in *S. 794. XXIX. Recurso de Hecho 'Solá, Jorge Vicente s. sucesión ab intestato', 12/11/1996,* published in *JA*, 1997-IV-654 with a note by Méndez Costa, María Josefa; CNCiv., Sala B, 23/02/15, *Van Hemelryk, Claudina Maria y otros s. información sumaria*, CNCiv., Sala B, 23/02/15.
83. Article 4, in both Protocols.
84. P. Lagarde, 'Public Policy', III *International Encyclopedia of Comparative Law*, *Private International Law*, Ch. 11, 7-3.

190. 'Manifestly', as written in the article, clearly reflects a difference. This adverb restricts the rejection of regularly applicable law to cases where the application is 'manifestly' incompatible with the principles and provisions of *OP*.

191. The difference deals with the limitation that CNG includes. The application of foreign law is rejected because it would require a manifest violation to local juridical order and principles.

192. However, *OP* is not the only barrier to the application of foreign law. Modern coding envisage different rules concerning OP and the application of imperative provisions as well as an exception clause to the application of foreign law due to the case's related actions with another order, a fact that can be explained in view of the different bases that support each hypothesis for not applying foreign law.

193. The new CCC is enrolled in this line in considering both institutions: the exception clause (Article 2597) and 'Internationally imperative rules' (Article 2599).

Article 2597 states that:

> *Exceptionally, the right designated by a conflict rule should not be applied when, on account of the set of factual circumstances, it is evident that the case has loosely relevant links to the law and, on the other hand, shows close links to the law of the other State, whose application is foreseeable and under whose rules the relationship has been validly established. This provision is not applicable when the parties have chosen the law for the case.*

In turn Article 2599 states that:

> *Internationally imperative rules, or those of Argentine law that are immediately applicable, are preeminent over the exercise of the autonomy of will and rule out the application of the foreign law chosen by conflict rule or by the Parties. When a foreign is applicable, its internationally imperative provisions are also applicable, and when it is required by legitimate interests, the effects of internationally imperative provisions of third-party States presenting close links manifestly predominant with the case may be recognised.*

§5. Evasion of Law

194. Fraudulent evasion of the law may be defined as the voluntary, malicious alteration of the point of connection laid down by the conflict rule with the aim of evading the coercive or imperative law applicable to the case. Thus two characteristic elements become manifest: voluntary evasion of a coercive right and the alteration of a point of connection with fraudulent intent.

195. The evasion of law is hereby used with fraudulent purposes. One type of evasion is the artificial manipulation of connecting factors to force Argentine courts to apply a legal system that differs from that which would normally apply. Examples are found in changing the domicile and the place of celebrating an act.

If the existence of fraud is determined, the corresponding sanction is non-application of the maliciously selected right, by virtue of the attempted manipulation, and the validity of the evaded right must be re-established.

196. The RCC did not contain a general rule sanctioning evasion of law, although it did include specific rules regarding contractual matters. Likewise, in matrimonial matters, the legislator expressly authorized – as does the current drafting of the code – spouses to move to another domicile in order to avoid submitting to the laws governing it, as *favor matrimonii* prevails over fraud.

However, the new CCC expressly regulates this institute in Article 2598. The rule says: *'To determine applicable law in matters involving rights not available to the parties, acts or facts carried out for the sole purpose of eluding application of the law designated by the conflict rules are not taken into consideration.'*

197. The Law of Commercial Companies includes a specific rule regarding fraudulent evasion of law. That rule of police, deals with the exclusive operation or exploitation in Argentina by a commercial company chartered in a foreign State. In those cases, the *lex fori* will apply exclusively (Article 124 CCL).[85]

198. The Argentine doctrine highlighted a notorious case of fraudulent evasion of law that regarded an Austrian citizen that was nationalized and had domicile in Argentina. When the citizen was diagnosed with a terminal illness, he moved back to Austria. There he nationalized Austrian again, and fixed his new domicile. The latter change in domicile had the purpose of enabling him to draft his testament giving the right to inherit to his fifth spouse and to exclude from those rights, without valid cause, all descendants from previous marriages.[86]

199. The above-mentioned rules should be questioned in the light of the existing jurisprudence. In most cases, the public policy exception attracted all cases where the fraud exception applied. In other words, there is limited authority as to which cases would fall under the scope of those specific rules.

200. The codifier (RCC) expressly authorized spouses to change domicile to avoid being subject to the applicable laws. Therefore, *favor matrimonii* prevails over fraudulent evasion of law in the law of marriage. Velez found inspiration in the work of Story, who depicted the struggle between two principles. On the one hand, the prohibition of fraudulent evasion of law; and on the other hand, *favor matrimonii*. The drafter regarded the latter in a paramount position. The fraudulent evasion of law is an oblique violation of the law. Even before divorce was recognized in Argentina, several court decisions rejected divorces entered into in foreign

85. *See* SCJN: *Compañía General de Negocios SAIFE s/ pedido de quiebra por Mihanovich L.*

86. CNCiv., Sala C, 03/03/81, *Mandl, Federico A. M. s/ sucesión*, *LL* 1981-C,63, with a comment by W. Goldschmidt.

jurisdictions.[87] The rule has not changed in the CCC; because of tradition more than necessity, the drafting remains the same.

201. The CNG stipulates that judges and authorities of States Parties shall enforce foreign law in the same way as they would be enforced by judges of the State whose law is applicable. That enforcement would be done without prejudice of the ability of parties to plead and prove the existence and content of the foreign law invoked (Article 2).

87. SCJN, 12/05/69, *Manuela Rosas de Egea*, *JA* 1969-III, 495 with a comment by W. Goldschmidt; CNCiv., en pleno, 08/11/73, *Martínez González de Zanotti, Marina s/ sucesión*, *ED* 54-136.

Part II. Choice-of-Law Rules

Chapter 1. Persons

§1. Natural Persons

I. Legal Capacity

202. The debate on whether every human being is a person has been settled since HRTs were given constitutional standing. Many HRTs include a clause stating that every human being is a person, i.e., every physical person has capacity of enjoyment and, as such, has rights and obligations.[88] Accordingly, all natural persons are recognized legal personality: are capable of having legal rights and obligations as well as being parties to legal proceedings.[89] These are some of the cardinal ideas the new CCC is founded on.

203. Domicile governs legal capacity according to the Argentine system. Legal capacity is one of the components of personal status that provides capacity or incapacity to perform legal acts. Nevertheless, in certain cases other connecting factors may be also relevant. For example, Article 159 CCC:

> The intrinsic and extrinsic conditions for the validity of a marriage are governed by the law of the place where it was contracted, even though the parties had left their domicile in order not to be subjected to the governing rules at such a place.

204. Article 948 CCC confirms the statements made by Vélez Sarsfield in Articles 6 and 7 of the same code. The former articles stated the capacity or incapacity of human persons domiciled in Argentina or abroad regardless of their nationality.[90]

205. Yet, some difficulties have arisen in the interpretation of Article 949, which referred to legal capacity or incapacity. Minors and persons incapacitated by a court

88. Two illustrations are found in Art. 6 of the Convention on the Rights of the Child, and in Art.15 of the Convention on the Elimination of All Forms of Discrimination against Women.
89. SCBs.As, 18/08/2010, *P.L., J. M. v. IOMA*, *LL* 22/02/2011, 4.
90. N. Lloveras & E. Faraoni, *La mayoría de edad en Argentina. Análisis de la Ley 26579* (Córdoba: Actualidad Jurídica, 2010).

order required approval of their acts by another person in order to perform binding legal acts. That rule established the application of *lex fori*. However, that legal category was an exception to the law of domicile applying to certain cases of incapacity to perform.

206. Ultimately, the capacity to perform, to have rights and obligations, to establish age, guardianship, parental authority, and absence were ruled by the law of the domicile. The latter, established the exact moment when legal personality begins and the condition of the conceived in the mothers' womb. However, exceptions to that rule were found in Article 159 RCC, which stated that the capacity to celebrate marriage is subject to the law of the place where it was contracted. In addition, Article 10 RCC established that the capacity to acquire or transfer immovables located in Argentina is governed by the laws of the country where the immovables are located.

207. Capacity acquired according to applicable law was not altered as a result of a change in domicile. Therefore, the principle 'once mature, always mature' applied. An exception to the general rule occurred when individuals that qualify as minors (or not emancipated) according to the law of a foreign domicile moved to Argentina, being in the latter considered of legal age. The exception was triggered by a change in the statute or movable conflict that established the decisive moment of the connecting factor in the current domicile. The spirit of the rule was to apply the most favourable law to the acquisition of capacity in a stage of transition (Article 138 RCC).

208. The same spirit was noticed in the subsequent article of the RCC. That article dealt with individuals of legal age (also emancipated minors) according to the law of the previous foreign domicile, but that were not considered of legal age by Argentine law. If those individuals established domicile in Argentina and have intention to stay, they were still considered of legal age, even when domestic law does not consider them as such.

209. Argentine courts rendered two paradigmatic decisions that followed that line of argument.[91] However, this situation currently continues to arise before local courts.[92]

210. The CCC has greatly simplified the regime provided for in the RCC. In this respect, Article 2616 provides that a person's legal and factual capacity and incapacity is governed by the law of his or her domicile, that is to say, the place Au: where he/she has settled physically. It also determines that a human person's change of domicile does not affect his or her capacity, once it has been acquired, regulating

91. SCJN, 13/08/1941, *Del Valle Inclán, Maria B.*, Fallos 190:354 and CNCiv., Sala C, 30/12/1957, *Berman, Evelina Geraldina Faustina*, *JA* 1958-IV-27.

92. CNCiv., Sala I, 31/08/04, *D., O. A. v. C., T. M. s. cesación de cuota alimentaria*, *ELDial* 06/10/04; Revista de Derecho de Familia N° 30 (March /April 2005), 211, with a comment by L.B. Scotti.

what is known as the 'irrevocability of the acquired capacity' in cases of mobile conflict.

211. Inspired by the principle of good faith, Article 2617 of the CCC in turn provides that a person entering into a legal act in a State whose laws consider him or her capable may not later invoke incapacity derived from the law of his or her domicile. There are three exceptions to this principle: the circumstances in which the co-contracting party knew or should have known of the incapacity; matters unrelated to international trade (family law and law of successions); and matters within the scope of *lex fori*, that is, the domestic law of the Argentine judge (real estate rights).

II. Name

212. The name of a person is considered a personal right, and therefore, is governed by the law of domicile. The Argentine law on names of persons (Law 18,248) from 1969 provided rules of control and was the rule followed until the CCC was enacted.

213. With the drafting of the novel legal order, a series of provisions were incorporated into Title 1, Chapter 4, dedicated to the human person, relating to names, surnames, name changes and actions, compatible with principles deeply rooted in universally recognized human rights and in a number of laws passed in recent years, designed to govern families.

214. In the field of PIL, the RCC contained no rules regarding the regulation of names. However, it is fitting to mention that the universal Human Rights movement raised the right to bear a name to the status of entirely personal, including it in the international conventions on the matter. As from then, qualifying a person's name as a personality right, gradually led to its being regulated as an autonomous category within the personal statute,[93] and this change of paradigm kicked off a reform process which, in Argentina, resulted in the inclusion of Article 2618 in the CCC, which provides that the law applicable to names is that of the domicile of the person involved, when it is imposed. Changing it is governed by the right of the person's domicile when it is required. Thus, for the first time in the history of the nation, autonomous PIL has a rule of conflict that determines the law applicable to names.

III. Nationality

215. Acquisition and loss of Argentine nationality is a matter of public or administrative law, and hence, does not qualify as an issue of PIL. Argentine Law 23,059

93. A. Ferreyra&A. Zavatti de Rougier, 'El nombre de las personas físicas y el Derecho Internacional Privado', *DJ* 2000-2, p.446.

regulates acquisition and loss of nationality, and replaced Law 346. The latter law had been overruled by Law 21,795, which had been subject to strong critics because of its approval without debate and for been contrary to the AC. The Law 23,059 repealed Law 21,795 and re-established the effects of Law 346 and its modifying laws (i.e., Laws 16,569; 16,801; 17,692; and 20,835). The Executive Order 3,214/84 implemented that law.

216. Two types of Argentine citizens derive from these provisions: (1) Argentine Natives. The category comprises those individuals born in the Argentine territory, whichever might be the nationality of their parents (with the exception of those born from foreign diplomats residing in Argentina); born in Argentine warships or foreign legations; and born in neutral seas (or airspace) subject to the flag of Argentina. This category also includes Argentine natives by option, that comprise those born in foreign countries from Argentine natives, and who opt for the citizenship of origin of their parents. This category finds grounding in the principle of *jus sanguinis* and requires that at least one of the parents be Argentine. This category differs from the Argentine by naturalization, because in the former the option is a right that cannot be denied, while in the latter, the right can be denied. (2) Argentine by Naturalization. This category comprises foreign individuals being over 18 years of age that reside in Argentina continuously for two years and claim before a federal judge that they want to be Argentines by naturalization. The two-year period may be shortened when the individual provides evidence of having served the interests of the country (Law 346, Article 2, paragraph 1).

217. However, nationality of human persons is determined according to the law of their State. Since July 2010, if persons have more than one nationality, they must not abandon one to obtain argentine nationality.[94]

218. Argentine nationality and citizenship are distinguished by law, and the latter settles the requirements for each case. If requirements are met, citizenship may also be acquired through naturalization.

219. The TMs have no regulations concerning nationality.[95]

IV. Change of Gender (Transsexuality)

220. Change of gender usually requires a change in the registered name and sex. There are no conflict rules concerning this issue in autonomous PIL.

94. Cám.Civ.Com.Fed.Plenario, 1/7/2010, Expte. N° 2775/2010, *Zunino Ignacio s/ petición, DJ* 15/7/2010.

95. M. Oyarzabal, *La nacionalidad argentina: Un estudio desde la perspectiva del derecho internacional público, del derecho internacional privado y del derecho interno argentino, con referencias al derecho de la integración* (Buenos Aires: La Ley, 2003).

221. Court decisions have favoured changes in name and sex, and allowed the requests. In addition, some courts rendered favourable decisions on transsexuality. The constitutional hierarchy of HRTs exerted a notorious influence in this area of law.

222. Regarding transsexuality, decisions authorized the implementation of surgery that would enable change of sex and ordered the delivery of new ID cards with the new identity. In the area of PIL, a case proceeded in which an individual, due to the prohibition in Argentina to undertake change of sex surgery, moved to Chile, where those surgeries are accepted by law. Once the surgery was performed in Chile, the individual returned to Argentina and requested before a court in Mendoza to implement a change in his name. The lower court rejected the claim, alleging a fraudulent evasion of law. However, the Supreme Court of the province modified the decision and granted the right to change of name.[96]

223. Regarding changes in gender, a court allowed the request from a man to become a woman without undertaking surgery for the change in sex. The grounds of the decision stated that the imposition of surgery would limit 'sex as gender by only one of its manifestations, that is to say, the presence of masculine external genital organs'. The court understood that the man should enjoy the same rights as a woman, and that Argentine institutions should accept him as such.[97]

224. Consequently, the OP with effects on PIL is modified by recognizing the change of gender to those domiciled in Argentina. The concept is re-examined and the foreign law of the state that allows the change is applied.[98] The novelty of Argentine jurisprudence is that there is no requirement of being of age if the circumstances needed for the authorization of the surgery are met.[99]

225. On 9 May 2012, the Congress of the Argentine Nation passed Law 26,743 on the person's right to gender identity, the finality of which is implicit in Article 1 of the law, which sets forth that all persons have the right to:

(a) Recognition of their gender identity.
(b) Freely develop their persona pursuant to their gender identity.
(c) Be treated in conformity with their gender identity and, in particular, be identified thus in the instruments that accredit their identity with regard to the first name(s), image, and sex recorded therein.

---

96. *See also*, Juzg. Civ. y Com. Córdoba, N° 19, 28/09/2001, *M.L. G. s/ acción de sustitución registral, LLC* 2001-1313.
97. Cám. Penal Mar del Plata, 16/03/2009, *S.E.L, LL* 2010-C, 312; Juzg.Fam. N° 8, La Matanza, *M., P.A. FYyP*, 2011.
98. C. Echegaray de Maussion &M. Lucero, 'Transexualidad y sentencia extranjera de reasignación de sexo: Cuestiones de derecho sustancial y procesal', *Actualidad Jurídica-Familia y Minoridad,* N° 60 (Córdoba: Ed. Nuevo Enfoque Jurídico, April 2009), 631.
99. A. Kemelmajer de Carlucci & E. Lamm, 'La persona transexual, menor de edad, competente para decidir sobre la intervención médica que requiere judicialmente', *Semanario Jurídico N° 1637* (Córdoba: T. 96, N° 23), 793.

§2. Juridical Persons

226. The identification of laws applicable to extraterritorial activities of juridical persons requires understanding of laws that apply to their existence. Cases in which foreign States perform acts as juridical persons are not challenging because the law of the place of incorporation and the law of domicile are the same. Article 146 subsection b of the CCC expressly provides that it recognizes as public juridical persons foreign States, organizations recognized by public international law as having legal status, and all other juridical persons incorporated abroad whose public character results from their applicable law. Subsequently, Article 147 provides that, as to their recognition, beginning, capacity, operation, organization, and end, public juridical persons shall be governed by the laws and legal orders of their incorporation.

Challenges arise with private juridical persons.

227. Conflicts may arise because private juridical persons can be incorporated in a country and have their domicile established in another. Therefore, it must be first resolved if a group has juridical personality and establish which law applies to that personality.

228. The RCC faced a gap in this respect, because there was no provision determining the law applicable to the existence and capacity of juridical persons. The application by analogy of Articles 118 and 124 (first part) Law 19,550 intended to solve the gap in the area of commercial companies.

229. However, that proposed solution encountered an obstacle. Article 124 is a rule of police, and it has been stated before in this presentation that these rules must be applied with a limited scope.

230. That gap must be solved because decisions must be rendered. Hence, according to the conditions of the case, references were made to analogous laws and general principles of law. In general, local doctrine favoured the application of the principle of domicile to the existence and capacity of juridical persons.

231. Today, Article 148 of the CCC lists private juridical persons: companies, civil associations, simple associations, foundations, churches, confessions, communities or religious entities, benefit societies, cooperatives, condominium consortiums and any other considered in the Code's provisions or other laws and whose character result from or is established by its finality or rules of operation.

232. In order to determine the applicable law, the new legislation distinguishes between those constituted in Argentina from those constituted abroad (Article 150).

The former are governed: (a) by the imperative rules of the special law or, failing that, by the CCC; (b) by the rules of their incorporation agreement, modifications and regulations; and (c) either the default rules of special laws or those of the CCC.

On the other hand, the same article now expressly provides that private juridical persons incorporated abroad are subject to the provisions of the CCL (Law 19,550).

233. In the conventional field, the Treaty of Montevideo on International Commercial Law (TMIComL) of 1889 (Article 4) states that existence and capacity of private juridical persons is governed by the law of the state of incorporation and recognition while the TMILComL of 1940 amended the connecting factor mentioned by the TMIComL of 1889, and favoured the law of domicile.

234. Both instruments clarify that their character fully enables them to exercise the actions and rights corresponding to them outside their place of incorporation. However, a restriction is established in exercising the acts embraced in their corporate purpose, in that they are subject to the provisions of the State in which they are to be undertaken. The 1940 TMILComL also demands that this exercise be habitual and extends the provision to civil societies.

Chapter 2. Obligations

§1. Law of Contract

235. An international contract has foreign elements. For example, the performance of a contract can be connected with a number of foreign countries or the domicile of one or both parties can be abroad. These contracts which are connected with different legal systems are currently considered one of the most relevant legal instruments of the international business dynamic.[100]

236. A large percentage of the economic activity of our globalized world materializes through international transactions. These transactions can be done through bilateral contracts (e.g., franchising, agency, business representation or leasing) or through partnership agreements (e.g., joint ventures).[101]

I. Autonomy of Parties (To Determine Proper Law)

237. The choice of law by parties deals with express and implicit choice of law. Parties freely decide if they enter into a contract and freely determine its content. The question is whether the implied or presumed intention of parties determines the proper law of the contract.[102] The principle of autonomy of parties is of fundamental importance with regards to international standard contracts. However, this principle is limited by the interaction of reasonable reliance and the justice or fairness exchange.

238. Autonomy of parties is analysed in light of freedom of contact. However, due to the evolution it encompasses, it is also of interest for PIL. Hence, an approach may concern the election of law, and is subdivided. On the one hand, autonomy before conflict rules which generates inquiries on the possibility to renounce to a connecting provision. On the other hand, autonomy before substantive provisions which generates inquiries on the feasibility to renounce to a material or substantive provision.[103]

239. Differentiation between party reference or choice of law and incorporation is needed. Party reference is an express or implicit choice of law that constitutes the connecting factor. Incorporation of foreign law may shape contact of parties as desired within the limits set by mandatory rules of the law that governs the contract.

100. *See*: A. Dreyzin de Klor. *La aplicación del derecho extranjero. Contratos internacionales. relaciones de consumo*, (Costa Rica: EJC. Serie monografías, 2015), 53.
101. *See*: Dicey, Morris & Collins, *The Conflict of Laws* 377 (Lord Collins of Mapesbury ed., Fourth Cumulative Supplement to the Fourteenth Edition, Great Britain: Sweet & Maxwell/Thomson Reuters, 2011).
102. *See*: C.M.V. Clarkson & J. Hill, *The Conflict of Laws* 170 (3rd ed., United States: Oxford, 2006).
103. *See*: J.A. Silva, *Derecho internacional privado* (México: Ed. Porrúa, 1999), 171.

240. Conflictual autonomy occurs when the chosen law is entirely applied, including both material and imperative rules. Accordingly, the choice of the parties is the connecting factor in the conflict provision and leads to the applicable legal order.

241. If parties had only substantive autonomy, they could only derogate material rules and not be able to derogate imperative rules of the applicable law. The latter law would be determined for each contract on the basis of another objective connecting factor.

242. The above-mentioned difference is relevant when determining whether mandatory rules of a legal system that would normally apply under the conflict rules of the forum are to be disregarded if parties agree to apply the law of another system.[104]

243. It is paramount that the validity of that reference is derived from the proper law of the contract and does not exceed the limits set by the substantive rules of that law. This is the case when freedom of parties is to be restricted to laws connected with the subject matter that arises only in connection with party references or when incorporation of parts of a legal system is not related to the matter.[105]

244. The question is to what extent parties are free to choose the law of the contract. Even before the current legislation came into effect, Argentine jurisprudence recognized autonomy of parties to determine the proper law of their contracts. Therefore, as stated before, parties were free to agree on the legal system that would govern their contracts, either the first or the second type of autonomy of parties.

245. Conflict autonomy and substantive autonomy may be instrumental in providing a greater ability to foresee results. In addition, it may assist in better regulate the contractual terms to be adapted according to the particular nature of the contract and to the requirements of the particular trade.[106]

It is relevant that parties may opt for the law of their contracts when considered adequate for their interests. This option may be made before celebration, at the time of conclusion, or later. Parties are even able to opt when appearing before courts. The choice of law may be retroactive, without detriment to the prevailing rights of third parties: a principle that must be respected by parties. The previous law governs the validity of the first contract, whereas its provisions are held subject to the subsequently chosen law. A change of the chosen law requires a new agreement, which will be governed under the same conditions of the first agreement.

104. O. Lando, 'Private International Law, Contracts', vol. III (K. Lipstein ed., *International Encyclopedia of Comparative Law*) 26-13.

105. *See*: O. Lando, *Private International Law, Contracts*, 13–14, §25.

106. *See*: A. Boggiano, *International Standard Contracts: The Price of Fairness* 151 (Dodrecht/Boston/London: Graham and Trotman/Martinus Nijhoff, 1991).

246. The choice of the proper law of the contract may be express or implicit. The chosen law made by parties requires a clear inference. Courts or arbitrators may infer from provisions of contracts or circumstances of cases that there are implied agreements between parties as to applicable law.[107]

247. There are conditions to recognize validity of choice-of-law clauses. Autonomy of parties provided in the law of contracts is only limited by the PIL system of the *lex fori*.

248. The main problem to determine is if it is recognized in the system, and if so, to what extent parties are free to choose the proper law of the contract.

249. Vélez Sarsfield's Code did not consider any form of expressing autonomy of will; however, because it is a universally accepted principle, as we have already anticipated, it had long been recognized by Argentine jurisprudence. The CCC, following the trend established as a rule based on the dynamics of international exchanges, expressly adopts the principle of autonomy of will, both conflictual and material.[108]

250. The current Article 2651 CCC provides that contracts are governed by the law selected by the parties as to their intrinsic validity, nature, effects, rights, and obligations. For such a choice to be valid, it must be expressed in, or emerge unequivocally from the terms of the contract and the circumstances of the case. The choice may refer to the whole of the contract or to parts thereof.

251. Exercising this right is subject to the following rules: (a) it can be agreed upon at any time that the contract be governed by a different law from that which it was formerly governed, either by a former choice or by the application of other provisions in this Code. However, this modification cannot affect the validity of the original contract or the rights of third parties; (b) once the application of a national law has been chosen, it must be construed that the domestic law of this country has been chosen excluding its conflict-of-law rules, unless otherwise agreed upon; (c) the parties may establish jointly the material content of their contracts and even create contractual provisions that displace coercive rules in the law chosen; (d) generally adopted trade usages and practices, customs and principles of international trade law, become applicable when the parties incorporate them into the contract; (e) principles of *OP* and internationally imperative rules in Argentine law apply to the legal relationship, irrespective of the law governing the contract; also imposed upon the contract, in principle, are internationally imperative rules of those States with overriding economic links to the case; (f) contracts drawn up in the republic in order to violate internationally imperative rules of a foreign country necessarily applicable to the case have no effect whatsoever; (g) the choice of a particular

107. J. Rivera, *Arbitraje comercial internacional y doméstico* (Buenos Aires: Lexis Nexis, 2007), 131 et seq.

108. *See*: A. Dreyzin de Klor, *La aplicación del derecho extranjero. Contratos Internacionales. Relaciones de Consumo* (Costa Rica: EJC, 2015).

national forum does not presuppose the choice of the domestic law applicable in the country in question. The rule clarifies that this prerogative in not applicable to consumption contracts (Article 2651).

II. No Choice of Law by the Parties

252. It is worth mentioning that to draft the rules formerly in effect, Vélez Sarsfield used the theories of Savigny and Story as sources. The theory of Savigny could be appreciated by the influence regarding the place of performance of contracts that have Argentine connection.[109] The theory of Story was seen when the codifier applied the law of the place of celebration of a contract as the most adequate, even when having no Argentine connection.[110]

253. Now the CCC provides that if the parties do not exercise the autonomy they are entitled to, the contract shall be governed by the law and the usage of the country of its performance. When it is not indicated or cannot be determined from the nature of the obligations, the place of its performance is the current domicile of the debtor obliged to deliver the service that most stands out in the contract. In the absence of these related circumstances, the contract shall submit to the laws and usages of the place where it was entered into. The new legal order also provides that contracts between absent parties be governed by the law of the State from which the accepted offer departs (Article 2652).

III. Legal Forms of Contracts

254. In the CCC, the regulation of the forms required by legal acts shall be judged pursuant to the laws and usage of the place where the acts were concluded. When the law that becomes applicable to the background of the international private legal relationship demands a particular form, the equivalence between said form and the form used shall be construed pursuant to the law of said country. If the contracting parties are in different States when entering into the contract, the form of the act shall be governed by the law from which the accepted offer came, or in absence thereof, by the law indicated to resolve the background of the international legal situation (Article 2649).

109. *See*: F.C. Von Savigny, *A Treatise on The Conflict of Laws and The Limits of their Operation in Respect of Place and Time* 221–222 (Trans. with Notes by W. Guthrie, 2nd ed. South Hackensack, New Jersey: Rothman Reprints Inc., 1972) and J. Story, *Commentaries on the Conflict of Laws, Foreign and Domestic, in Regard to Contracts, Rights, and Remedies* (Boston Hilliard, Gray and Co., 1834).

110. *See also* the study by A. Parise which identifies the different references that the Argentine codifier made to the works of Story. A. Parise, 'Legal Transplants and Codification: Exploring the North American Sources of the Civil Code of Argentina (1871)', in Gutiérrez Posse et al., *Informes de la Asociación Argentina de Derecho Comparado* (Buenos Aires: XVIII Congreso de la Academia Internacional de Derecho Comparado, 2010), 267–338.

IV. Breach of Contracts

255. The law of contract governs the breach of the agreement, i.e., it governs the breach of a fundamental term of the contract. However, parties may incorporate conditions that specifically regulate circumstances that would amount to a relevant breach. Furthermore, they may also incorporate special clauses to determine the effects of breaches they consider relevant.

V. Multilateral Treaties

256. In the conventional dimension, the TMs of 1889 and 1940 use the place of performance as connecting factor. Autonomy of parties is expressly prohibited in Article 5 Additional Protocol to Montevideo Treaties (APMT). The latter states that the intention of the parties does not modify the rules of legislative and judicial competence described in the Treaties. Even when the provision states that it may only act within the scope provided by competent law. The last paragraph has been subject of doctrinal debate, and Argentine courts must accept it when a conflict rule refers to a legal system where conflict autonomy is admitted.[111]

257. Contracts are governed by a series of analytical solutions because autonomy of parties is neglected when choosing the applicable law. Those solutions enable the legislator of the convention to establish the place of performance of a contract (Articles 36–42 Treaty of Montevideo on International Civil Law (TMI-CivL) 1940).[112]

258. MERCOSUR, as codification forum for institutional PIL, provided the framework for the adoption of a Protocol on International Contractual Jurisdiction. The articles of that Protocol expressly allow the prorogation of jurisdiction, either by compromise or by an arbitration clause.[113] Therefore, it indirectly enables the determination of applicable law.[114] The limit to choose jurisdiction is that written agreements are not entered into in an abusive way.

111. *See*: M. Albornoz, 'As for the 1940 Montevideo Civil International Law Treaty and the additional Protocol, party autonomy rejection or reception depends on whether we *see* the glass half empty (rejection) or half full (restricted reception)', *Choice of Law in International Contracts in Latin American Legal systems* (Mexico: Cide, 2009).

112. CNCiv., Sala G, 09/08/89, *Smulevich, Alberto y otro v. Disi, Roberto y otros, ED* 139-708; SCJN, 26/12/95, *Méndez Valles, Fernando v. Pescio A. M. s/ ejecución de alquileres, LL* 1996-C, 499-507, with comment by G.J. Bidart Campos.

113. MERCOSUR/CMC/DEC No. 1/94: Protocol of Buenos Aires on International Jurisdiction in Contractual Matters.

114. CNACCF, Sala 1, *Robinsa SA v. Rolando SA*, 26/04/2004, in 'Segundo informe sobre la aplicación del derecho del MERCOSUR por los tribunales nacionales', Secretaria MERCOSUR (Montevideo: Konrad Adenauer Stiftung, 2004), 242.

§2. PARTICULAR CONTRACTS

I. Contracts for Sale of Goods

259. Argentina ratified the Convention on Contracts for the International Sale of Goods (CISG). Contracts for sale of goods in Argentina results from the interplay of three conventions: CISG; New York Convention on the Limitation Period in the International Sales of Goods of 1974; and the Protocol amending the Convention on the Limitation Period in the International Sale of Goods of 1980.

260. The universally accepted CISG applies even without request of parties when conflicts fall within its material and jurisdictional scope (paragraph 33 *supra*, indicated that treaties prevail over the autonomous dimension of parties). CISG has been also vastly welcomed by the jurisprudence.[115] For example, a case rendered by a Court of Appeals on 24 June 2010 accepted the claims of the plaintiff and reversed the decision of the lower court. The judge of the lower court, applying domestic law, stated that even when there was a breach of contract on behalf of the defendant, the facts mentioned in the petition did not suffice to generate a compensation for damages because they did not provide enough evidence. It was stated that even when the plaintiff invoked CISG, the petition did not comply with the provisions of the treaty. The argument of the plaintiff found specific grounding in the application of CISG and its principle of compensatory action.[116]

II. Employment Contracts

261. There is no specific legislation regarding employment contracts in PIL. The jurisprudence applies domestic law to the international employment contracts. For example, the Argentine Labour Court of Appeals, through a substantiated resolution, applied Articles 1215 and 1216 CCD to deny a request for prorogation of jurisdiction in favour of a foreign State.[117]

262. The provisions of Labour Law are deemed public policy. Consequently, every agreement between parties that eliminate or reduce rights that are prescribed by law (or other special provisions or collective agreements) is null and void.[118]

115. A. Garro & M.P Perales Viscasillas, 'Opiniones del CCIM-AC: Consejo Consultivo en materia de compraventa internacional de mercancías', *DeCITA* 9, 2008, CEDEP, 14–78.

116. CamNacAp, *Sanovo I.S.A v. Ovoprot I.S.A s/ Ordinario*, with comments by C. Harrington, 'Responsabilidad por incumplimiento en la compraventa internacional de mercaderías', *RDCO*, 2011. An application of Art. 1, inc. b) of CISG is found in a ruling of the same court ratifying the universal acceptance of CISG. *See Ecotune (India) Private Ltd. v. Cencosud SA s/ ordinario*, Judgment of 7/10/2010.

117. CNTrab., 18/09/2008, *Verdaguer Ricardo Anibal v. IMPSAT Fiber Networks Inc. y otro s/ despido*, www.diprargentina.com.

118. R.Chares Laver, *The Legal System of Argentina*,vol. 10, 10–20, 62–63 (K.R Redden ed., *Modern Legal Systems Cyclopedia*, USA: William H. Hein & CO, 1994).

III. Insurance Contracts

263. With the exception of the provisions that rule marine insurances, Argentina has no autonomous rule in this field.[119] These provisions rule the suitable jurisdiction and not applicable law. Therefore, marine insurance agreements do not allow accords between parties regarding jurisdiction and the prorogation of jurisdiction is only allowed once the fact that generates the controversy takes place.

264. This kind of contract is a particular type that is regulated by each State. Insurance companies have a function concerning the scope of activities determined by specifically mandatory rules, forming part of a category of contracts which are typically commercial and usually of adhesion. This category of contracts has a limited territorial scope covering risks situated in the State and witnesses the disparity between insurance companies and beneficiaries. This disparity results from the close connection of the regulation of the activity with the economic politics of States, affecting in many cases the contractual terms.

265. The applicable law to international insurance contracts is one of the most complex matters of contemporary PIL. This complexity derives from the current relevancy of insurance contracts since it is not possible to conceive an import/export operation without suitable insurance contracted by the buyer, the seller, the carrier, or the provider of services.[120]

266. In the conventional dimension, the TMILComL (1940) refers to land insurance. It recognizes international jurisdiction to the courts that according to the parallelism of forums have their laws applied. The connecting factor is the domicile of the insurance companies (or that of their branches or agencies). Alternatively, it recognizes jurisdiction to judges of the domicile of the insurance companies (Article 13).

267. The law of domicile of insurance companies (or that of their branches or agencies) applies to life insurance. Other land insurance are governed by the law of the State where the goods where located at the time of celebration (Article 12).

268. The TMILComL of 1940 establishes that in flight and marine insurance the jurisdiction will be that of the domicile of the insurance companies (or that of their branches or agencies). In the event insurance companies initiate claims, they can opt for the jurisdiction of the domicile of the insured (Articles 30 and 43).

269. Land and marine insurance are governed by the law of the State where the goods where located at the time of celebration of the contract.

---

119. Articles 620 and 621, Law 20,094.

120. A.L. Calvo Caravaca & J. Carrascosa González (eds), *Derecho internacional privado*, Vol. II, 14ª ed. (Granada: Comares, 2013), 777 y ss.

270. The Protocol of Buenos Aires – MERCOSUR – especially excludes the insurance contract. However, freedom of circulation is a requirement for integration, and hence, some provisions on insurance have been established. For example, Resolution 120/94 GMC, adopted in Argentina by Resolution 23,875 of the National Agency of Insurance – Superintendencia de Seguros de la Nación (S.S.N.), intends to harmonize the provisions regarding civil liability of the owner or driver of a vehicle (leisure automobiles or rented cars) not registered in the country of destination with regards to the damages caused to persons or not transported goods.[121]

IV. Consumer Contracts and E-Commerce

271. The RCC did not regulate contracts entered into with consumers. The current law on consumer protection[122] also does not make reference to e-commerce, and there are no provisions regarding that contractual practice. Argentina did not enter into conventions or documents drafted in international codification forums.[123]

272. Notwithstanding, and in view of the fact that the consumer has gained prominence worldwide, the new CCC incorporates the category as an independent and specific contractual type.[124] This attitude reflects the example emerging from modern legislations that uncovers the philosophical conception of this figure.

273. Article 2654 regulates the competent jurisdiction in the matter, conceding a considerable number of alternative forums so that the acting consumer may opt based on his or her convenience in view of his or her vulnerability in this legal relationship. In this direction, the rule considers that the lawsuit may be filed in the jurisdiction where the contract was entered into, where the service is performed, where the goods are delivered, where the compliance guarantee was undertaken, the place where the consumer makes the necessary acts to conclude the contract, or the

---

121. C. Harrington, 'Transporte benévolo y seguro de responsabilidad civil del MERCOSUR: un caso para la reflexión', in *RDPC*, 2009-2 (Santa Fe; Rubinzal Culzoni, 2009), 283.
122. Law 26,361 (*BO* 7/4/2008). The new law does not incorporate provisions regarding the applicable law to consumer contracts. However, it does incorporate changes in, amongst others, procedure, implementation of direct and punitive damages, extension of the concept of consumer.
123. *See*: C. Lima Marques, 'Confiança no comércio eletrônico e a proteção do consumidor (un estudo dos negócios jurídicos de consumo no comércio eletrônico)', *Revista dos Tribunais*, Brazil, 2004. Also M. Lucero de Godoy & C. Echegaray de Maussión, 'La protección internacional del consumidor. Algunas propuestas para una codificación regional', in *Protección de los Consumidores en América*, trabajos de la CIDIP VII (OEA), (Asunción: La Ley Paraguay S.A. - Centro de Estudios de Derecho, Economía y Política –CEDEP-, 2008), 347/360, and Ricardo L. Lorenzetti, *Consumidores*, 2da. ed. (Argentina: Rubinzal Culzoni, 2009).
124. *See*: A. Dreyzin de Klor (Director) / I. Ellerman (Coordinator), *Los Derechos del Consumidor. Visión internacional. Una mirada interna*, Zavalia, Buenos Aires, 2012. and Lima Marques C., 'La insuficiente protección del consumidor en las normas del Derecho Internacional Privado – De la necesidad de una Convención Interamericana (CIDIP) sobre la ley aplicable a algunos contratos y relaciones de consumo', in: *La Protección del consumidor: aspectos de Derecho: aspectos de derecho privado regional y general*, Cursos de Derecho Internacional Privado, Serie temática, vol. I (parte 2): El Derecho Internacional Privado en las Américas (1974–2000), Washington D.C, Comité Jurídico Interamericano. Secretaría General, OEA, 2002, p. 1518.

jurisdiction of the judges of the State in which the defendant has a subsidiary, agency or any kind of commercial representation, when these have taken part in concluding the contract or when the defendant has mentioned them for the purposes of complying with a contractual obligation.

The rule about international jurisdiction considers an important number of attributive forums, a scope that clearly shows to what extent legislators have assumed the need to protect consumers, providing them with a wide variety of options to bring action against suppliers.

274. Such that when legal action is brought against the consumer by the other contracting party the only forum in which the lawsuit may be filed is that of the judges of the State of the consumer's domicile. The contracting parties may not evade the jurisdiction laid down by law, given the fact that it is forbidden to extend the jurisdiction of this type of contract (Article 2654).

275. In the field of the law applicable to consumption contracts, Article 2655 of the CCC provides that these shall be governed by the law of the consumer's domicile. This connection is used provided the rules consigned throughout the four hypotheses listed in the rule are observed. ((a) If conclusion of the contract was preceded by an offer or some publicity or activity carried out in the State of the consumer's domicile, and the consumer has complied with the necessary acts to conclude the contract therein; (b) if the supplier has received the request within the State of the consumer's domicile; (c) if the consumer was induced by the supplier to move to a foreign State to place the order from there; and (d) if the travel contracts include combined services of transportation and lodging for a global price.)

276. Whereby if the circumstances indicated are not duly configured, the contract shall be governed by the country of its performance and only in the hypothetical case in which the country of enforcement cannot be specified shall the contract be subject to the law of the place it was entered into.

The key rule that becomes the axis around which the regulations adopted revolve is the banning of freedom of choice. This stance is based on a protective policy, which leads to the adoption of rules materially oriented towards protecting consumers; such rules necessarily emerge from the analysis of the specificities typical of such relationships, namely, informative imbalance, discontinuity, mass supply, and difficulties.[125]

125. C. Lima Marques, 'La insuficiente protección del consumidor en las normas del Derecho Internacional Privado – De la necesidad de una Convención Interamericana (CIDIP) sobre la ley aplicable a algunos contratos y relaciones de consumo', en: *La Protección del consumidor: aspectos de Derecho: aspectos de derecho privado regional y general*, Cursos de Derecho Internacional Privado, Serie temática, vol I (parte 2), El Derecho Internacional Privado en las Américas (1974–2000), (Washington D.C.: Comité Jurídico Interamericano. Secretaría General, OEA, 2002), p. 1518.

V. Contract of Carriage

277. The term 'contract of carriage of goods' is usually used to describe the transportation of specific goods. The basic obligation is to deliver goods that have been carried from a port of loading to a port of destination.[126]

278. The definition states that there is an obligation related to the desired purpose (i.e., of results), the latter being to comply with the transportation of goods from one place to another and to deliver them to the addressee or consignee. The carrier will undertake the risks that relate with the act of transportation until the delivery is performed.

279. Autonomous PIL does not include conflict rules on transportation by land.

280. Jurisprudence applies the provisions of the RCC (Articles 163, 164,167,171, and 205). The latter have been developed to rule on local matters. The decision of the SCJN in the case '*Compte v. Ibarra*' is certainly influential in this area. Since that decision, Argentine courts are deemed competent in claims that derive from contracts of carriage to be performed in Argentina, even when the usual clauses of shipping indicate a foreign court.[127]

281. Marine transportation is addressed in the Admiralty Law 20,094 (modified by Law 26,354), which dedicates a chapter to PIL.

282. The Admiralty Law determines that the nationality of the ship is given by the use of the flag. Accordingly, it will rule all matters related to the law of the flag. The principle of reciprocity will apply for the validity of property rights and mortgages charted abroad. Hence, the change of nationality will not affect the privileges and other existing property rights. The law of the flag also governs the powers, duties, and attributions of the captain. The retainer agreements of the crew, captain, and officers are governed by the law of the state where the ship renders service. Therefore, they are all subject to that law.

283. The law of the state where the contract is performed (i.e., the place where the render of merchandise was agreed) governs charter agreements and transportation of goods agreements shipped under bills of landing or general loadings.

284. Argentina is a Member State of the Brussels Convention of 1919 on Salvage of Aircraft at Sea. Consequently, due to that ratification, this Convention applies to related cases.

285. Air transportation is regulated by the Argentine Aeronautic Code. That code includes in Title XI a section on 'applicable law, jurisdiction, and competence'.

126. J.D. Ray et al., *Transport Law* 59 (*International Encyclopaedia of Laws*, Supl. 22, The Hague: Kluwer Law International, 2007).
127. SCJN, 16/11/36, *Compte y Cía. Soc. v. Ibarra y Cía. Soc.*, Fallos 176:218.

Even when it does not include specific rules on transportation agreements, it grants jurisdiction to national courts in cases referring to air circulation and airport operation. In addition, it states that Argentine law applies to acts that take place in the country and to acts and crimes that take place in Argentine ships in Argentine territory or in the international airspace not subject to foreign claims of sovereignty. This regulation is silent on contracts of transport by air; hence, the gap is completed by the provisions that apply to contracts in general (Articles 2651/2653). Jurisdiction will be ruled by the provisions of Article 2650.

286. Law 24,921 (*BO* 12/01/1998) regulates the multimodal transportation of goods, both locally and internationally. The scope of application is limited to having the parties established in the contract the place of delivery within Argentine jurisdiction.

VI. Leasing/Factoring/Franchising

287. Argentina adopted the Law 25,248 on leasing. However, this law does not contain provisions related to PIL. Most contractual cases before Argentine courts had a substantive connection with Argentina because it was the place of celebration or performance. Consequently, Articles 1209 and 1210 RCC were the applicable law in this matter.

288. In an operating or finance lease, the place of performance needs to be defined. Scholars state that the contract is first governed by the autonomy of parties, both regarding conflicts (i.e., to choose the applicable law) and matter (i.e., to incorporate derogative clauses of coercive domestic provisions of the country whose laws apply). Subsidiary, the contract will be governed by the law of the place of performance, which will be the current domicile of the debtor of the most distinctive service.

289. The goods that are subject to international leasing may be acquired by the holder at the moment of termination. The only condition is to pay the import-taxes not paid at the time the goods entered the country.

290. International leasing is currently gaining importance due to its flexibility to deal with the problematic of dynamic international business. For example, the accounting of exportation (either done at the state of the seller or at the state of the buyer) protects parties against currency fluctuation. It is mainly an agile and effective mechanism of finance and technology for small and mid-size business.[128]

291. Import/export factoring contracts are presumed to be located in the State of the domicile of the general agent (i.e., Factor), when applicable law has not been stated by the parties in the contract, the criteria of localization is based in the place

128. *See*: A. Sierralta Ríos, *Negociación y contratación internacional* (Lima: Legis, 2007), 507.

of performance understood as the domicile of the debtor of the most distinctive service. There is international jurisdiction in the court chosen by the parties or in the courts of the domicile of any of them.

292. Franchising has long been an integral part of the globalization of business and an important tool in the development of investments. Unfortunately, even when contemplated in different Civil and Commercial projects, Argentina currently has no rules regarding franchising. For example, the revision project of 1998 deals with the contracts of agency and concession, and states that the provisions applicable to concession contracts will be applied, when appropriate, to distribution contracts.

§3. Non-contractual Obligations

I. *Lex Loci Delicti*

293. *Lex loci delicti* refers to the liability that derives from a significant number of situations; for example, those derived from product liability; unjust enrichment; *negotiorum gestio;* use of nuclear energy; car, train, ship, and vessel accidents; intellectual property infringements; and antirust.

294. Regrettably, autonomous PIL was silent is this respect. That silence generated a serious problem when determining how to bridge that gap in the important area of international torts.

295. A look into comparative legislation reflects that a position has been adopted. Amongst the many possibilities, the applicable law will be that of the place of the crime, where the goods are bought, where the effects take place or that of the common domicile of the parties.

296. The CCC expressly regulates the competent jurisdiction and the law applicable to the criteria of extracontractual liability. Concerning jurisdiction, it provides that actions for damages deriving from different facts related to breach of contract are to be brought, opted for by the actor, in the law courts of the country of the defendant's domicile, in those of the place where the fact causing the damage occurred, or in those where the resulting harmful effects occurred (Article 2656). The law regulating the resolution of cases of public liability is that of the State where the damage is done. However, if the actor and defendant have their domiciles in the same country, the law of the State where they both reside may be applied, regardless of where the damage was done (Article 2657).[129]

297. The TMILComL of 1889, in the area of conventions, states that obligations that arise from non-contract sources are governed by the law of the State where the

129. *See*: A. Dreyzin de Klor & I. Ellerman, 'La evolución de la responsabilidad civil extracontractual en el DIPr: a propósito de la sanción del nuevo Código Civil y Comercial de la Nación', *La Ley online:* AR/DOC/4036/2015.

actions – licit or illicit – from which they derive took place (Article 38). Fifty years later, upon its revision, the rule is completed by stating that they will be ruled by the law that governs the juridical relations to which they obey (Article 43). The latter is because the illicit act may result from another pre-existent juridical relation amongst the parties, and would then be connected to the law of that previous situation.

298. The doctrine developed by Argentine experts in the X Congress of the AADI[130] states that the wording of those articles does not prevent innovative and autarkic qualifications regarding the 'place where the act took place'. That doctrine includes in that concept not only the place where the action is manifest but also where the consequences take place.

299. Court decisions reflect that most tort cases derive from car accidents pertaining Argentina and Uruguay. Therefore, it is no surprise that it has been included in the conventions and provisions of institutional standing (MERCOSUR). This is reflected in the Protocol of San Luis on Civil Liability Resulting from Traffic Accidents between Member States of MERCOSUR.

300. Argentina and Uruguay signed the Bilateral Agreement on Civil Liability arising from Traffic Accidents, which is in force since 8 June 1995. The convention determines not only the applicable law in cases of civil liability arising from traffic accidents that take place in the state where the persons are domiciled and in the State where it has effects, but also in the international jurisdiction.

301. *Lex loci delicti comissi* was adopted in the provision. That principle applies when persons are domiciled in both States. However, an exception refers to accidents where only persons domiciled in the other State participate or are affected. In this situation, it will be governed by the internal law of that other State.

302. When dealing with the impact of MERCOSUR and the Protocol of San Luis on applicable law, experts find difficult the application of *lex loci actus* to cases of torts in which an accident is the only connecting factor with Uruguay. Moreover, that difficulty is faced when the solution is related to the domicile of the defendants, which also settles jurisdiction. The application of the social scope of the parties was seen more fair than the application of the law of Uruguay, which was one of the place of the accident. There is clearly a tendency towards the application of the law that is common to the parties over the *lex loci.*[131]

303. The Protocol of San Luis is certainly a new ground for the jurisprudence, because it modified the positions since it took effect. The jurisprudence is divided when applying the Protocol. Therefore, in two similar cases related to traffic accidents in Uruguay, Argentine courts followed different standings regarding applicable law. The agreement is silent regarding the time of application and does not

130. Held in Buenos Aires in 1989.
131. SCJN, 24/09/1969, *Sastre, T. v. Bibiloni, F.N. y otro*, Fallos 274:455.

contain clauses dealing with the TMs. Accordingly, in one of the cases, the judges applied the Protocol even when it was not effective at the time of the accident.[132]

304. Notwithstanding, in another case, the possibility to refer to that agreement was expressly denied because the latter was not effective at the time of the accident. The international jurisdiction of Argentine courts found grounding in the domicile of the defendant. The Court of Appeals stated that regarding applicable law the coexistence of the TMs and the Bilateral Agreement between Uruguay and Argentina raised a time problem for the unfolding of provision of PIL. The court considered necessary the study of the provisions of VCLT because the rule of conflict of laws or of conflict of jurisdictions belonged to an international treaty. Therefore, the problems of transitory law that could be generated would be subject to international law at large.[133]

305. Differences between the two instruments (Bilateral Agreement and Protocol of San Luis) are visible at a glance. The solution provided by the traditional position is in decline. Court decisions reflect that the tendency is to adopt criteria that adapts to specific matters in tort cases, aiming to equilibrium by the harmonization of individual and common interests.

II. Unjust Enrichment

306. All patrimonial attributions must have a cause. The RCC did not provide a systematization of provisions on unjust enrichment. However, both doctrine and jurisprudence evidently claimed its regulation.

307. Today the CCC contains two articles that provide expressly that anyone who becomes rich with no lawful purpose at the expense of another is obliged to compensate, to the extent of his or her profit, the patrimonial detriment of the impoverished party (Article 1764). In turn, it provides that this action is not appropriate if the aggrieved party has some other means of obtaining compensation for the impoverishment (Article 1765).

308. Although the topic is not specifically regulated, the general provisions in the matter of public liability (Articles 2656/2657) and their application to different circumstances shall be followed in resolving such cases.

---

132. CNCiv., Sala L, September 23-996, *Giuliani, Mario y otro v. Khafif, Isaac y otros*, *LL* T.1998-C.
133. CNCiv., Sala I, 14 Apr. 1998, *Rivas Cordero, Santiago v. Natanson, Jorge o Gustavo Jorge Osvaldo s/daños y perjuicios*, *ED* 182,752.

Chapter 3. Property Law

§1. General Rules

I. *Lex Rei Sitae*

309. *Lex rei sitae* is the law of the place where the property is located and determines the acquisition, transfer, and extinction of rights on immovable property. Almost universally, that law establishes the substance, exercise, and effects of the acquisition and loss of property rights.

310. In the Argentine system of autonomous PIL, *lex rei sitae* applies to the above mentioned. In addition, either on movables or immovables, it indicates what rights in assets are recognized, how in rem rights are created and terminated, whether there are formalities to be complied with, and what benefits are enjoyed *erga omnes* by the holder of the right. Real rights are specifically enumerated in domestic private law (Article 1887 CCC).

311. The underlying rationale for this rule is justified on the basis of the particular interests the State has on lands. A public policy rule relates to this autonomous conflict-of-law rule, thus the domestic regulation prevails over other laws.

312. That provision results in contracts concerning rights on immovables being subject to mandatory requirements of form according to Argentine law. The legal system establishes the transfer of consent of parties by both registration and delivery. The consent must be done by an agreement specifying the proprietary aspects of the transaction, and it must be done before a public notary. Public interest motivates the accuracy of land registry.

313. *Lex rei sitae* also applies to movable property that is a mere accessory to other property or to those objects that the owner has no intention to carry.

314. This is a noteworthy rule that applies subsidiary when a thing has no owner due to being abandoned, due to ignorance on who the owner is, or due to being a thing lost by its owner. A court decision followed that criteria when dealing with foreign currency found on a ship docked at an Argentine port, and decided that it would be considered as located in Argentina.[134]

II. Movables and Immovables

315. Savigny and Story were sources for the Argentine codifier Velez Sarsfield in the area of property. Regarding goods, Savigny adopts the law of the domicile of

134. CNCC, Sala D, *D'Argenar S. As.*, 16/09/63, *LL* 112–313.

the owner and Story the law where the goods are located. Notwithstanding, given that both provide exceptions to their principles, the application of their theories have the same outcome.

316. Section 15 of the new CCC regulates what are called real rights. Article 2663, based on Article 10 of the RCC, provides that the classification as an immovable is determined by the law of the place where it is located. Real action on immovables is in turn brought exclusively before judges of the place where the asset is located (Article 2664). It is an exclusive forum for real action on immovables located in the Argentine Republic that reasserts the regulatory, doctrinal, and case law tradition prevailing in the country.

317. Concerning registered movables, Article 2665 considers that real actions on registered movables must be brought exclusively before the judges of the State of the Registry. The jurisdiction for lodging real action on non-registered movables is concurrent, given the fact that the actor may choose to file the lawsuit before the judges of the defendant's domicile, or before the judges of the place where the goods are located (Article 2666).

318. With regard to the law applicable to the real rights on immovables, the new legal order provides that they be governed by the law of the place where they are located (Article 2667). Real rights on registered movables are governed by the law of the State of the Registry (Article 2668). Real rights on movable goods whose situation is permanent and which are conserved and not intended to be transported are governed by the law of the place where the goods in question are located when the legal action is brought. Rights thus constituted are valid even when the property is subsequently moved to another State (Article 2669).

319. The TMs do not distinguish between movables and immovables. The *lex rei sitae* is the general rule for protection of rights on corporeal or material goods.

III. Transfer of Property

320. The CCC provides rules on contracts entered into in foreign States to transfer real rights on immovables located in Argentina. Thus, it provides that contracts drawn up in a foreign country to transfer real rights on immovables located in the Republic have the same force as those drawn up in the State's territory, provided they are recorded in public instruments and are submitted legalized (Article 2667).

321. The law of the place where the document is produced will determine the qualification of a public document.

§2. SPECIAL RULES

I. Predial Servitudes in Different Countries

322. The jurisprudence, for over fifty years, has favoured the servient estate when servitudes have dominant estate and servient estate in different countries.[135]

II. Mortgages

323. Instruments issued in foreign States to create mortgages over property located in Argentina must comply with the same requirements of form and registration expected in cases of transfer of immovables located in Argentina.

324. It is clear that the document is formally registered, yet not the obligation. Mortgages created in Argentina are different with regards to the time when they produce legal effects. Those mortgages, if registered in a timely manner, produce effects on third parties since the day the mortgage obligation is granted. Mortgages created in a foreign State and registered within the six-day period since the judge requires formal registration, will have effects since the request for formal registration is approved at court.

325. According to the TMs (TMICivL) of 1889 and 1940, *lex rei sitae* governs real rights of mortgage and pledge (Articles 26, 1889; and 32, 1940).

III. Goods in Transit (*Res in Transitu*)

326. The CCC provides that real rights on movable property, that is to say, what the owner always carries with him or her for personal use, and goods that are for sale or transportation, shall be governed by the law of the owner's domicile. When this domicile is unknown or contested, the law of the place where the property is located shall apply (Article 2670).[136]

135. *See*: Busso & Petracchi, *Código civil anotado*, T. I, Art. 10 – No.39 (Buenos Aires: Ediar, 1945).
136. *See*: A. Dreyzin de Klor, *Código Civil y Comercial de la Nación Comentado*, Tome XI, Arts. 2666–2671. Modificaciones a las Leyes 17.801, 19.550 y 24.240, R.L. Lorenzetti, Director, (Argentina: Rubinzal Culzoni Editores, 2015), p. 671.

Chapter 4. Intangible Property Rights

327. As starting thought, is worth mentioning that 'rights of intellectual property' includes two categories: copyright and industrial property rights. Copyright includes rights on literary, artistic, or scientific works. Industrial property rights include rights on patents and utility models, as well as trademarks and commercial trade names which are characterized by a business impact on those rights. Both rights recognize the fundamental need to protect the 'creations of the mind'.

328. Notwithstanding the regulations particular to every institute, it should be emphasized that the provision contained in Article 2609 of the CCC which, when listing the cases of exclusive Argentine jurisdiction, besides cases dealing with real rights on immovables located in the country, includes disputes relating to the validity or nullity of registrations made in a public registry and on matters of registrations or the validity of patents, trademarks, designs or drawings, when the deposit or registration was requested or effected or taken to be effected in Argentina.

§1. Copyright

329. Copyright is governed by Law 11,723. In Article 12, the law states that intellectual property is governed by the provisions of the law that is common, and according to the limits and conditions available in the law. In addition, it has three rules on foreign works of art that can be summarized as follows:

- Protection of literary works published abroad should be recognized in Argentina without distinguishing nationality of the author, if the latter comes from a State that recognizes intellectual property rights.
- To enjoy the benefits of the law, authors of foreign works must give proof of performance of formalities in the country in which the publication was originally made.

330. The protection to works of art of foreign authors cannot be broader than the one given in the country of origin. However, if foreign laws give broader protection than Argentine law, the latter will govern.

331. There are no current rules stating jurisdiction for international cases. A specific procedure applies to civil claims originated due to application of the law or due to juridical acts celebrated within its framework (Article 80), and this finds grounding in the provisions on dilatory pleas that procedural codes provide.

332. From the conventional perspective, Argentina ratified regional and international agreements.

The following agreements are in force in the regional level:

- Treaty on Literary and Artistic Property, Montevideo.
- Convention on Literary and Artistic Copyright, Buenos Aires (Law 13,585, *BO* 27/10/1949).
- Inter-American Convention on the Rights of the Author in Literary, Scientific and Artistic Works, Washington (Law 14,186, *BO* 24/7/1953).

The following agreements are in force in the international level:

- Convention for the Protection of Literary and Artistic Works, Berne (Laws 17,251 and 25,140).
- Universal Copyright Convention, Geneva (ratified by executive order 12,088/57).
- International Convention for the Protection of Performers, Producers of Phonograms and Broadcasting Organizations, Rome (ratified by executive order 23,921).
- Convention for the Protection of Producers of Phonograms against Unauthorized Duplication of Their Phonograms, Geneva (Law 19,963).
- Convention Establishing the World Intellectual Property Organization (WIPO), Stockholm (Law 22,195).
- Treaty on the International Registration of Audiovisual Works, Geneva (Law 24,039).
- Agreement on Trade Related Aspects of Intellectual Property Rights, Uruguay (Law 24,425).
- WIPO Copyright and related rights, Geneva (Law 25,140) (WCT).

333. Most legal instruments mention that the law of the place where the protection is claimed will govern. This law will determine the extension of the applicable law and the cause of action to be claimed. The above-mentioned international conventions helped to harmonize the standard of protection for these rights. Notwithstanding, in domestic law, the principles of territoriality and domestic ruling prevail. The second principle implies a non-discriminatory obligation towards the artistic work of foreign authors.

334. Currently, it is not possible to talk of extraterritoriality of the rights of the author. Whenever authors want to protect works of art in a country different from that of original publication, they must comply with the requirements established by the law of the new place of publication.[137]

§2. Patent Law and Trademarks

335. Argentine Patent Law 24,481 (1995), amended by Law 24,572 (1996), states that physical persons or national or foreign juridical persons can obtain the

137. *See*: D. Lipzyc, *Nuevos Temas de Derecho de Autor y Derechos Conexos* (Buenos Aires: Zavalia, 2004).

protection of intellectual property rights if they establish in Argentina a domicile determined for that legal purpose.

336. Trademark Law 22,362 (1980), without making references to nationality, also states that authors need to establish domicile in the city of Buenos Aires for legal purposes. Accordingly, authors (physical or juridical persons) with a foreign domicile will have to establish jurisdiction in Argentina in order to receive legal notice on nullity or expiration of trademarks.

337. Industrial models fall under the scope of executive order 6,673/1963. The principle of reciprocity applies since the law recognizes to authors of foreign industrial models equivalent rights to those in Argentina. To achieve equal recognition, the law of the foreign author of the industrial model must recognize industrial models of Argentine authors. Notwithstanding, the above-mentioned rule lost gravitation when Argentina ratified the Paris Convention for the Protection of Industrial Property (Law 17,011) and the WIPO/OMPI World Intellectual Property Organization (Law 24,425, *BO* 5/01/1995).[138]

§3. Rights of Personality

338. Rights of personality may be characterized as part of the personal status and therefore subject to the law of the domicile. These rights refer to the right to life, physical integrity, and personal and family honour. Therefore, protection of personality rights is not dealt within conflict-of-laws rules. However, international conventions on human rights due apply because rights of personality concern human rights. Nonetheless, from a conflict-of-laws perspective, the violation of such rights results in civil liability cases to which choice-of-law rules on torts apply.

138. CNCivComFed., Sala I, 12/08/2010, *Peters Hnos. Cia. Com. e Ind. S.A. v. Institut National des Appellations D' Origin*, *ElDial*, 12/2/2011.

Chapter 5. Company Law

§1. Introduction

339. Argentine autonomous PIL mainly provides conflict-of-law rules to corporations and other commercial companies incorporated in foreign States. These juridical persons are regulated in section XV, CCL under the title 'On Companies Incorporated Abroad'.[139]

340. The material scope of that section governs the capacity of action and the conditions that rule foreign companies that intend to make business in Argentina.

341. These rules are vitally important because their application extends to legal entities in general since, as the CC provides in Article 150, private juridical persons incorporated abroad are governed by the provisions of the CCL.

§2. Applicable Law

I. Place of Incorporation

342. Article 118 CCL sets the general choice-of-law rule on the law applicable to foreign companies. The *lex societatis* is the law of the state of incorporation of the company. This law governs existence and types of companies.[140]

343. The juridical concept 'form,' also covers publicity and incorporation: means of authentication of the act to be registered and publicized, and the effects that incorporation and publicity generate. Therefore, it is also the law applicable to the assessment of the ineffectiveness of what was not registered or publicized.

II. Activities of Foreign Companies

344. Foreign companies, according to Argentine law, may perform isolated acts of commerce in Argentina.[141] However, foreign companies must comply with a series of formalities if they intend to perform in a regular basis acts that compose their corporate purpose.[142] In addition, foreign companies must comply with the provisions of Article if they intend to settle a branch, agency, or any other means of permanent representation.

---

139. Law 19,550 and modifying laws. Section XV: *'De la sociedad constituida en el extranjero'*.
140. A. Boggiano, *Curso de Derecho internacional privado. Derecho de las relaciones privadas internacionales*, 591.
141. CCDCom.Rosario, Sala III, 13/03/2007, *Club Atlético Newell's Old Boys*, *LL* Litoral-2007 (July), 676 - IMP 15 Aug. 2007, La Ley online: AR/JUR/806/2007.
142. Juzg.Nac.1°Inst.Com., N°10, 13/08/2009, *Consorcio de Prop. Edificio de la calle Ecuador 1320 esquina Charcas v. Casaucic S.A.*, *DJ* 17/02/2010, 371, La Ley online: AR/JUR/33298/2009.

345. Accordingly, foreign companies could attempt to incorporate a company in Argentina. In order to do so, they must ascertain before a judge of the Office of Incorporations that they comply with laws of incorporation of the countries of origin. In addition, they must register their contracts of creation, existing amendments, and all documentation relative to their permission to operate, together with the information regarding their legal representatives. Registrations must be done, according to their nature, before the Public Commercial Registry or the National Registry of Joint-Stock Companies.

346. There are three requirements according to the law. (1) There must be proof of the existence of the company according to the laws of the country of incorporation. (2) There must be a domicile established in Argentina and must comply with the requirements of publicity and incorporation of the *lex fori* for companies established in the country. (3) There must be valid reasons for the incorporation in Argentina and a person must be appointed to operate the company. When a branch is established, interested parties must also indicate the capital according to special and applicable laws.

347. Conflict-of-laws rules also provide answers to cases of incorporation in foreign countries pursuant to types of companies unknown in Argentina. In those cases, judges must establish the requirements matching them with the highest standards provided in the Argentine legislation.

348. Those companies must keep separate accounting books in Argentina and be subject to the controls applicable to corresponding types of companies.

III. Liability of Representatives and Judicial Summons

349. The law states the same liability for acts of designated representatives and local administrators. When dealing with types of companies not regulated in Argentina, the standard is higher because it is levelled with the liability of directors of stock companies.

350. Judicial summons to foreign companies is twofold: (i) it arises when it is generated due to an isolated act within Argentina; or (ii) it arises when the foreign company has a branch, agency, or any other means of permanent representation. In the first case, the law states that the summons must be made on the agent that participated in that act or contract that generated the claim. In the second case, the summons must be made on the representative.[143]

---

143. CNCom., Sala F, 08/07/2010, *Consumidores Financieros Asociación Civil p/su defensa v. Crédit Suisse*, La Ley 09/08/2010, 2010-D, 642, *La ley online*: AR/JUR/36344/2010; CNCom., Sala A, 23/02/2010, *Golub, Gustavo v. International Vendome Rome-Ivr S.A.*, La Ley 14/04/2010, 14/04/2010, 11 – *LL* 2010-B, 671 – *LL* 27/08/2010, 4, with comment by Lisandro A. Allende; Mariana A. Miglino; *LL* 2010-E, 82; *La ley online*: AR/JUR/4505/2010.

IV. Liability due to Bankruptcy

351. The violation of liability rules of Argentine company law may trigger liability of representatives when facing bankruptcy of companies they represent (Article 121, Law 19,550; Article 173, Law 24,522).[144/145] According to domestic law, once bankruptcy of foreign companies is ruled in Argentina, the representatives of those companies may be deemed liable.

V. Fraudulent Evasion of Law

352. Fraudulent evasion of law by a foreign company is governed by a rule of police of the CCL. If the main purpose of the foreign company is indented to be performed in Argentina, the legislator will treat that company as local with regards to the fulfilment of incorporation formalities, reform, and control of operations.[146]

§3. Conventional Dimension

353. The conventional dimension is completed by the TMIComL of 1889 and TMILComL of 1940, which were followed by Conferencias Interamericanas sobre Derecho Internacional Privado (CIDIP) II of Commercial Companies (CSC). The latter overrules the provisions on companies of the TMILComL because it was ratified by Argentina, Paraguay, and Uruguay.

354. In general lines, the solution is the same under the treaties of applicable law to the performance of commercial companies duly incorporated in a state. The connecting factor shall be the law of the place where they are incorporated.

355. The law of the place of incorporation governs the existence, capacity, operation, and termination of commercial companies.

356. The expression 'law of the place of incorporation' must be understood as the law of the State where the formal and substantive requirements for the establishment of a commercial company are fulfilled. This rule triggers problems in cases of incorporation in multiple States, and they all can claim to be the place of incorporation. Some scholars understand that the company must be considered a unity of association, and therefore, apply the law of the state where the decision-making

144. CNCom., Sala A, 20/08/2009, *Bratar S.A. v. Rocca, Bernardo E, JA*, 20/1/2010.
145. *See* E.H. Richard, 'Actividad ilícita de sociedad extranjera (indirect doing business) y su quiebra en el país (en torno a importantísimo fallo de la Corte)', *ElDial Express*, 16/3/2009.
146. Juzg.Nac.1°Inst.Com., N°10, 13/08/2009, *Consorcio de Prop. Edificio de la calle Ecuador 1320 esquina Charcas v. Casaucic S.A.*, *DJ* 17/02/2010, 371, *La Ley online*: AR/JUR/33298/2009; CNCom., Sala E, 07/10/2008, *Representaciones de Telecomunicaciones S.A.*, *LL* 07/05/2009, 6, with comment by Alejandro Drucaroff Aguiar; *LL* 2009-C, 308; La ley online: AR/JUR/24351/2008.

organs of the company are located.[147] Other scholars understand that the natural and unique place of incorporation is that where the company was first registered.[148]

357. Once formally incorporated in one state, companies will be acknowledged in other Member States. However, recognition does not preclude a foreign state from requiring proof of existence of commercial companies in accordance with laws of the place of incorporation.

358. The capacity of a company as juridical person does not include, preliminarily, the capacity to act. That capacity to act is governed by the provisions that deal with the extraterritorial activity of companies.[149]

359. According to the Treaty, the capacity of foreign commercial companies will never be broader than the capacity of commercial companies incorporated pursuant to domestic law.

360. *Lex societatis* governs rights and duties of partners, together with all other aspects of the operation of companies. *Lex societatis* also governs the interactions of headquarters of companies with their branches. Finally, that same law also deals with the modifications to the contract that creates the companies.

361. When foreign commercial companies intend to establish their headquarters or main place of business in another state, they may be required to fulfil with the requirements of the laws of the country where they decide to do business.

362. The CSC includes a provision (Article 6) on jurisdiction that reads:

> For the performance of acts directly or indirectly incidental to their purposes, commercial companies constituted in one state shall be subject to judicial or administrative authorities of the state where they perform such acts.

§4. Trusts

363. Trusts do not exist in Argentine law. This is not only the case in Argentina, because many other civil law jurisdictions find it also unknown.

364. However, if a foreign commercial company creates a trust with a foreign bank, and that bank has a branch in Argentina that recruits investors domiciled in Argentina and abroad, that commercial transaction will be protected by Article 118 CCL because the foreign law of incorporation will govern the personal law of the

147. A. Boggiano, *Sociedades y grupos multinacionales* (Buenos Aires: Depalma, 1985).
148. D. Opertti, 'El problema de las sociedades comerciales extranacionales en el derecho internacional privado (en especial en la doctrina)', in *Temas de derecho internacional privado*, N° 4, 33.
149. Opertti, 'El problema de las sociedades comerciales extranacionales', 29–51.

company. A stock trust agreement will exist whenever the principal purpose of the company is not aimed to be performed in Argentina. As long as the international *OP* is not violated, it may be alleged that it is an unknown institution, and the relative provisions would apply without rejecting the stock trust agreement.

Chapter 6. Bankruptcy

§1. General Regime in Autonomous PIL

365. The regime in force for autonomous PIL is provided by Law 24,522, amendments, and related provisions.[150]

366. Debtors domiciled or with administrative headquarters in Argentina[151] and debtors with foreign domicile can enter into preventive remedies before domestic courts regarding property located in the country. 'Debtor' comprises all physical or private juridical persons, corporations where Argentina is partner, and the patrimony of deceased individuals as long as it can be separated from the patrimony of heirs.

367. When the debtor is domiciled abroad, the judge of the country of the administration of the company will have jurisdiction. If it is not possible to determine the latter, Article 3 states that the court with jurisdiction is that of the country where the company is located, operates, or has its principal activity.

368. Only in the event of the lack of a business headquarters for the bankruptcy of the natural person shall the competent judge be that of his or her domicile, which is based on the publishing nature of the procedure in the interests of protecting the correct exercise of the creditors' rights, and of the different parties' numerous interests.[152]

369. The law states that if debtors undergo preventive remedies in foreign countries, they may initiate preventive remedies also in Argentina. In these cases, debtors or local creditors must submit petitions in Argentina. Local creditors are those creditors whose debts must be cancelled in the country.[153] Argentina will therefore recognize the initiation of foreign preventive remedies abroad as a cause for petition in the country. However, this recognition will be limited to requests from those mentioned in the provision.[154]

370. The first paragraph of Article 4 provides that the declaration of insolvency abroad is a cause for opening the insolvency in the country, upon request of the debtor or creditor whose credit must be made effective within the Republic. It is worth noting that the possibility of ordering a bankruptcy in the country caused by

150. BO 9/8/95, last amendment: Law 26, 086, BO 11/4/2006.
151. CNCom., Sala A. 02/10/09, *Bendelman, Ana s/ pedido de quiebra por Gutiérrez, Juan Alberto, La Ley Online:*AR/JUR/46140/2009.
152. SCJN, 31/05/2005, *Gowland Carlos Luis s. quiebra*, Fallos 328:1797, citado en autos CNCom., Sala F, 19/05/2011, *Tavelli Augusto Martin s. pedido de quiebra por Espiño Andrés José, www.diprargentina.com.*
153. A. Rouillon, 'Cuestiones de Derecho internacional privado en la ley concursal argentina 24,522', in *Anales de la Academia Nacional de Derecho y Cs. Sociales de Bs. As.* 1999, year XLIV, N° 37.
154. CNCom., Sala D, 24/11/2010, *BII Creditanstalt International Bank Ltd. s/ pedido de quiebra promovido por Vizcaino Jose*, *ElDial.com* 15/03/2010.

a universal process of liquidation of assets abroad, leads the national insolvency to be derived abroad, but independently and autonomously, as the opening declared in Argentina does not involve the 'exequaturization' of the foreign declaration.[155]

371. When bankruptcy is also declared in the country (multiple bankruptcies), foreign creditors can only pursue the balance after creditors claimed in the domestic bankruptcy. Legislation recognizes the international treaties in Article 4 which states that 'foreign bankruptcy cannot go against creditors whose credits are to be paid in Argentina, in order to dispute rights claimed over goods existing in the territory nor to cancel acts celebrated by the debtor'. Therefore, the legislator adopted the principle of favouring nationals, either in original or derived bankruptcy proceedings. That principle states that creditors with interests to be performed in Argentina have privilege over those creditors with interests to be performed abroad.

372. Reciprocity is also welcomed.[156] The claim of creditors whose interests are to be performed abroad and that are not part of a foreign bankruptcy proceeding must give proof that a similar claim would be welcomed in their country of origin under same conditions as the ones they intend to claim in Argentina.

373. Finally, a note is worth regarding the cancelling of foreign unsecured credits claimed after bankruptcy proceedings initiated in Argentina. In those cases, they will be deemed as part of the dividends applicable to creditors that hold general credits, while creditors with securities will not be required to give proof of reciprocity.

§2. Treaties of Montevideo

374. Bankruptcy is dealt with in the TMILComL of 1889 in Articles 35–48, while the TMIComL of 1940 provides a more extensive chapter, extending from Articles 40 to 53. It is important to add a reference to Articles 16–25, TMIPL 1940, which relate to preventive remedies. The TMs of 1889 is silent with regards to remedy proceedings and the provisions that govern international bankruptcy apply by analogy. The TMICivL of 1940 includes a provision that enables the application of the rules of bankruptcy to judicial liquidation or settlement of accounts, preventive remedies, suspension of payments, or other similar situations included in the laws of Member States.

375. Three problems arise from the provisions of this conventional dimension. The first problem relates to the territoriality or extraterritoriality of the fact that

155. M.E. Uzal, 'Panorama actual de la regulación de la insolvencia en el Derecho comparado. Análisis de la posibilidad de aplicación extraterritorial del art. 4 de la Ley 24.522', *ED.*, T. 172, 910.

156. SCdeMza., Sala I, 28/4/2005, *Sabaté Sas S. A. en Covisan, P/conc.,LL* 2005-D, 247, with comment by M.E. Uzal. In an untimely claim, foreign law was even applied by own motion of the local court.

generates the bankruptcy, and needs to determine if the court declaration of bankruptcy in one country generates automatically similar declarations in other Member States. The second problem deals with the unity or plurality of bankruptcy proceedings. The third problem deals with determining if treaties provide for unity or plurality of bankruptcy estates.

376. Regarding the first problem, both treaties adopt the principle of extraterritoriality of the generating fact. Once bankruptcy is declared in one country, it must proceed in all other Member States. Regarding the second problem, there is an understanding that there is only one bankruptcy proceeding if the insolvent party holds commercial offices, even through branches or agencies in different countries, and even when in the latter the insolvent rarely undertakes acts of commerce. Conversely, if the future insolvent party holds two or more independent and autonomous commercial offices in different territories, single or multiple bankruptcies might proceed according to the amount of commercial offices. Regarding the third problem, the unity or plurality of bankruptcy estates will derive from the unity or plurality of proceedings.

377. To further clarify the above mentioned, it may be stated again that bankruptcy declared in one state produces similar extraterritorial effects as those of foreign court decisions. The latter applies to, amongst others, publicity, precautionary measures, and recognition of the authority of receivers of the bankruptcy proceeding. The property of the insolvent that is located in other Member States will be subject to the precautionary measures that were established by the judge that declared the bankruptcy. Moreover, authority is recognized to foreign officials, receivers, or administrators of the bankruptcy proceedings that undertake similar functions to the ones of the place where the bankruptcy was declared. These foreign appointees may implement precautionary measures, administer, and appear in court during the proceedings.

378. Precautionary measures and publicity may be implemented by international letters rogatory. The letters rogatory will enable the judge of the bankruptcy proceeding to request from the judge where the property is located to implement restraining orders to prevent the selling of property or similar actions according to the provisions of each legal system.

379. The TMs adopt a system of plurality of bankruptcy estates or of privilege for domestic creditors regarding goods located in the country where credits are to be paid. This position is logical in cases of plurality of bankruptcy estates. However, in the system of the TMs, even in cases where only one bankruptcy exists, the product of that proceeding will be separate in estates to favour creditors with credits payable in the same place where goods were located.

380. The TMs (1889–1940) grant international jurisdiction to the court of the commercial domicile of the debtor, either if the debtor is a physical person or a company.[157] The jurisdiction will persist even if the debtor holds branches or agencies in other States and when these depend on the principle branch. If the debtor holds independent commercial offices in different States, jurisdiction will fall on the judges of the domicile of each office.

157. In the previously mentioned case *Compañía General de Negocios pide la quiebra Mihanovich, Ricardo L.* of 2009, the SCJN stated the criteria of effective commercial domicile for off-shore companies. That decision was followed in the case *Fortleitsar*, CNCom, 27/4/2010.

Chapter 7. Family Law

§1. Introduction

381. Argentine PIL is inspired and guided by HRTs. These treaties incorporated principles of equality, non-discrimination, and identity to the AC. Even when those rights were tacitly incorporated before the reform of 1994, since then, they have been expressly included in the CC. Family law, in all its manifestations, is the area of law most influenced by the reform of 1994. Family as an institution is considered the nucleus of society and base of its construction and development. Today, the debate even extends to the recognition of its existence as such. Notwithstanding, its institutional characteristic is not threatened. The latest amendments re-define the concept giving birth to a large number of systems that co-exist in the social universe.[158] The new CCC is a good example of the above mentioned.

382. The discrepancies that overcame with the last reform fortified the nuclear family by changing the traditional concept and raising questions. They helped better understand that not all families are identical, yet they all need to be recognized, to enjoy rights, and to be protected by a juridical framework.[159]

383. The incorporation and recognition of juridical effects to civil unions involves a vast number of figures that percolate through this aspect of contemporary juridical science. Some of those figures are: same-sex marriage; assisted reproduction; gestational surrogacy; adoption of a child by a homosexual or heterosexual partner of one of the biological or adoptive parents; family composed by one parent; and assembled families.[160] The heterogeneity of the previously mentioned institute leads directly to frame the concept of family within the postmodern perspective of PIL, which is based on values such as plurality and respect of cultural identity.[161] This intensifies the need to analyse the juridical relations and the connections that overcome to correctly consider a number of situations that are not subject to rule or that need adequate regulation. For a number of years, Argentina has been undertaking the task of redrafting its legislation in order to harmonize the system to the constant changes it experiences. An analysis of the entire legislation was needed to regain a juridical system dealing with family and including the current contextual complexities in which domestic private law and domestic PIL develop.

---

158. *See*: K. Boele-Woelki, *What comparative Family Law Should Entail?* 4(2) *Utrecht L. Rev.*1–24 2008.
159. A. Dreyzin & C.E. Echegaray de Maussion (eds), *Nuevos Paradigmas de Familia y su reflejo en el Derecho Internacional* (Córdoba: Ed. Advocatus, 2011).
160. A. Dreyzin, 'Los principales desarrollos dentro del Derecho Internacional Privado en el próximo siglo en Argentina', *Revista Mexicana de Derecho Internacional Privado, Número Especial* (México: D.F., 2000).
161. E. Jayme, 'O directo Internacional Privado e a Familia no umbral do Seculo XXI', in *Cadernos do Programa de pós-graduacao en directo – PPGDIr./UFRGS*, Vol. 1, N° 1, (Porto Alegre: Universidad Federal de Río Grande do Sul, March 2010).

384. The new CCC, enrolled in constitutionalizing private law, has contributed significantly to the democratization of the family and has given occasion to 'family rights', which results in providing comprehensive protection without remaining anchored to a traditional view of the family.

The prevailing broad conception includes plural manifestations with similar, though not identical, characteristics; thus for example, cohabitational union is recognized by domestic law as an institution that produces legal effects, and therefore autonomous PIL, coherent with the evolution of the national normative system, also provides a solution to the jurisdictional problems that could result from the bonds between common-law-partners.

385. From that perspective, and since there is a sort of equivalency amongst States due to grounding of provisions in common essential principles, it is no surprise to identify an autonomous PIL highlighted by similar axioms. This area, similarly to the rest of the law, results from changes in society. Therefore, it is affected by constitutional changes, something that does not occur with the opening of new markets or migrations and their impact on family law.

§2. Unmarried Couples

386. Cohabitational union was not systematically and normatively received in Argentina until the new CCC was enacted, although before this domestic legislation recognized some effects derived from this figure,[162] because as it exists in the form of factual unions, as a social reality, its effects could not go unrecognized.

This institution currently enjoys express legal recognition in domestic law and, although it is similar to marriage in that the configuring elements are similar, the difference of the founding act is a relevant reason that merits differentiated legal treatment. The same happens in the context of autonomous PIL.

387. Article 2627 provides that any actions referring to the validity of the cohabitational union or its personal effects or assets must be undertaken before the judges of the State where the members of the union live together and where their life is centred or, by choice of the actor, before the judges of the defendant's habitual domicile. Meanwhile, the law that regulates both the conditions of validity and the personal effects and assets deriving from the cohabitational union is that of the State where the parties invoke its validity (Article 2628).

162. The following can be mentioned as examples: continuing the rental contract in favour of the renting common-law-partner (Art. 9, Law 23,091), the right to a pension in favour of the common-law-partner (Law 23,570), the presumption of the cohabitant's fatherhood (Art. 257 of the RCC), among others. For this point, *see*: A. Dreyzin de Klor, *El derecho internacional de familia en la postmodernidad*, (Costa Rica: Editorial Jurídica Continental, 2012), p.18.

§3. MARRIAGE

388. Marriage is based on the principles of equality and non-discrimination. In addition, the institution is notoriously affected by the spirit of HRTs.

389. Equality comprises the spirit and rules included in the HRTs. However, in this specific situation, it means that neither the state nor an individual may discriminate on grounds of sexual orientation. The previous definition of marriage regarded as a union between a man and a woman has been correctly left behind.

390. A long path was followed in order to adopt the current definition. First, when the RCC was adopted, marriage was defined as the indissoluble union of one man and one woman for life to the exclusion of all others.[163] Such definition was based on the catholic concept of marriage, but there have been several statutory reforms to that rule over the years. Once divorce was incorporated in the domestic legislation, the character of indissolubility abandoned the paramount position. Currently, since the law reform introducing the equality between men and women, there is no requirement of different gender for spouses. Heterosexual and same-sex couples currently enjoy the right to marriage.

I. Validity (Capacity and Form)

391. Marriage is ruled by the law of the place of celebration according to the conflict rule. In addition, it expressly allows spouses to change domicile in order to be governed by a different law to that which governs their jurisdictional statute (Article 2622). This rule currently lacks of relevance because marriage is no longer indissoluble and heterosexual. However, the same wording has prevailed through the different amendments. Tradition has kept that wording, because it was motivated by *favor matrimonii* in times when the jurisdictional statute imposed prohibitions that did not exist in other States. (Article 2622). The primacy of the point of connection 'place of celebration' over the right that should be applied according to the personal statute of the spouses on one hand, and the exception of evasion of the law on the other, clearly show the legislators position towards strengthening the principle of *favor matrimonii.*

392. However, *lex loci celebrationis* is upheld insofar as the situations described in the second paragraph, which assume the nature of an internationally imperative rule or police rule, are not configured. Consequently, grounds for kinship, bond, and crime appearing in the rules to which the article alludes specifically (Article 403, subsections a, b, c, d, and e; and Article 575, second paragraph) act as an impediment for recognizing a marriage celebrated abroad.

163. Marriage pursuant to the original provisions of the CCD was reformed in 1888, with the adoption of the Law 2,393. In 1987, the Law 23,515 introduced divorce. In 2010, the Law 26,618 (15/07/2010, *BO* 22/7/2010) introduced same-sex marriage.

The situations considered are: consanguinity between relatives in the ascending or descending line, between siblings or half siblings, the bond derived from adoption, as well as direct relatives in all degrees. Further grounds for precluding recognition of a marriage celebrated abroad are those which result from the bond existing from having undergone assisted human reproduction techniques (AHRT), which are assimilated to full adoption. In addition to these grounds are preclusions based on the existence of an earlier marriage and mariticide, both picked up by the internationally imperative rule in comment, which is considered of matrimonial *OP*.

Notwithstanding, *lex loci celebrationis* prevails as long as the public policy situations are not met. The impediments refer to relationship, existing marriage, and murder of spouse.

393. The law of celebration of marriage governs both the conditions for intrinsic and extrinsic validity. Proof of marriage is also governed by the law of the place of celebration.[164] That same law governs the validity conditions of the direct and supplementary evidence.

394. In Argentina, Law 26.618 – enacted on 15 July 2010 –, which modifies the RCC, allowed marriage between people of the same sex. Therefore, public policy was modified and marriages entered into abroad between persons of the same sex and same-sex civil partnerships are recognized in the Argentine Republic.

395. Although case law relative to same-sex marriages celebrated abroad and requesting recognition in the country is scarce, the Supreme Court ruled in domestic cases that reflect the criterion adopted by the country on the matter. It indicated that:

> It is inofficious for the Supreme Court of Justice of the Nation to rule on the federal issue raised, relative to the unconstitutionality of articles 172, 188 and concordant and complementary articles in the Civil Code, in that they establish the requirement of heterosexuality to marry before the enactment of law 26,618 of equal marriage, which no longer considers this restriction, as the Courts rulings must address the circumstance existing at the time of the decision, even though they survive the federal action being brought.[165]

In this sense, it is the ruling whereby it is claimed that:

> Given the fact that the Supreme Court of Justice of the Nation's rulings must address the circumstances at the moment of the decision – even though they survive the federal action being brought – it is consider the issue abstract for

164. CNCiv., Sala I, 11/11/2004, *B. M. N. v. Agea S.A.*, *La Ley Online*: AR/JUR/4502/2004; CNCiv., Sala F, 17/06/1998, *Durante, Eugenio s/ suc.*, La Ley 1999-A, 180 - DJ 1999-1, 205.

165. SCJN, *María de la Cruz Rachid and other v. National Registry of Marital Status and Persons' Capacity*, 24/08/2010, 30/08/2010, *La Ley* 2010-E, 105, Cita online: AR/JUR/44017/2010.

the Court to rule on the federal issue raised in the case, relative to the unconstitutionality of articles 172, 188 and cc. of the Civil Code, in that they establish the requirement of heterosexuality to marry, before the enactment of law 26,618 of equal marriage, which nlo longer considers this restriction, whereby the matter should be declared abstract.[166]

396. In relation to the form of marriage, the Argentine system conceives a solemn act that requires for its validity the manifestation of consent in a certain form and with intervention of an officer of the Civil Registry before witnesses. The consent of spouses provides the material grounding for the validity of marriage. The intrinsic validity is governed by the law of the place of celebration, and the latter also governs the effects of apparent or imperfect consent due to error or lack of free consent by the spouses.

397. Consequently, the notion of marriage is reinforced by the HTRs because the existence of consent is a principle of *OP* included in those treaties of constitutional hierarchy.[167]

398. The legal capacity to marry is when a person attains 18 years of age. Parental consent is required for marriages of persons under that age and never before married.[168]

399. Argentine public policy does not allow marriage in cases of consanguinity amongst ascendants and descendants, amongst siblings and half siblings, amongst those subject to relations derived from adoptions, and amongst those with affinity in direct line in all degrees. Existing marriage[169] and murder of spouse are public policy impediments to celebrate marriage.[170]

400. Proof of marriage is regulated by the law of the country in which the union is celebrated. With regard to this point, it is relevant to mention that case law has expressed that the fact of a marriage celebrated abroad is governed by the law of the place of its celebration, 'it cannot be concluded therefrom that it follows that the interested party is bound to show that the certificate attached to the trial is in

166. SCJN, *V., A. J. and other v. National Registry of Marital Status and Persons' Capacity*, *La Ley* online: AR/JUR/44015/2010.

167. N. Lloveras & M. Salomón, *El Derecho de Familia desde la Constitución Nacional,* 105.

168. Law 26,449 unified the legal age as 18 years for women and men. The law was enacted on 3 Dec. 2008 and published in the Official Gazette on 5 Jan. 2009.

169. SCJN, 12/11/96, *Solá, Jorge Vicente s/ sucesión ab intestato*, *JA* 1997-IV, 654, with comment by M.J. Méndez Costa. In that case, the court found grounding in the variability and current nature of OP when deciding favourably on the validity of a marriage celebrated in Paraguay by a person previously married in Argentina and divorced pursuant to Law 2,393 (with no dissolution of marriage bond). That doctrine was then followed in numerous decisions since the adoption of Law 23,515. Regarding this leading case, *see also* SSJN, 14/09/10, *Boo, Héctor José s/ sucesión testamentaria*, www.diprargentina.com and SCJN, 10/04/07, *Ulloa, Alberto s/ sucesión*, *SJA* 12/12/07, with comment by S.L. Feldstein de Cárdenas and M.S. Rodríguez.

170. CNCiv., Sala I, 12/11/02, *F. Y. y otro s/ sucesión ab intestato*, *LL* 2003-D, 445.

accordance with the law of the aforementioned place of celebration'.[171] It should be observed that rulings delivered by Argentine courts establish the rule's scope, where it is this law, in turn, that governs the conditions of validity of the direct and supplementary evidence.

II. Marriage at a Distance

401. Argentina allows the celebration of marriage at a distance. This provision was incorporated to the RCC before the adoption of Law 23,515. Argentina signed the Convention on Consent to Marriage, Minimum Age for Marriage and Registration of Marriages of New York of 1962.[172] Notwithstanding, some differences can be recognized between both sets of rules. Accordingly, the place of consent, which fulfils the act, will be considered the place of celebration. The place of celebration will be defined following the *lex fori* juridical concept and the form of the act will be governed by the *lex loci.*

402. The CCC provides that a distance marriage is considered to be that in which the absent party expresses his or her consent, personally, before the competent authority for authorizing marriages in the place of his whereabouts. The documentation accrediting the absent party's consent may only be offered within ninety days of the date on which it was drawn up. Distance marriage is considered to have been celebrated in the place where consent is given. The competent authority in celebrating the marriage must verify that the contracting parties are not affected by any legal impediments and decide upon the reasons alleged to justify the absence (Article 2623).

§4. Dissolution

I. Annulment

403. Annulment of marriage is governed by the same law that rules its validity. It may be requested if any of the impediments that violate OP are encountered.

404. The CCC establishes that any action related to the validity, nullity or dissolution of the matrimonial institution, or its personal effects or assets, must be brought before the judges of the state where the spouses lived together before their separation or, by choice of the actor, before the judges of the domicile or habitual residence of the defendant (Article 2621).

405. The SCJN decided in a case filed in Argentina (pursuant to the domicile of the spouses) claiming the annulment of a marriage celebrated in Paraguay. The court

171. CNCivil, Sala I, 11/11/2004, *B. M. N. c/ Agea S.A.*, *La Ley* online: AR/JUR/4502/2004.
172. Law 18,444, 13/11/1969, *BO* 24/11/1969.

decided that it would imply a significant limitation to rights of the plaintiff to reach a decision on the substance of her petition and stated that a decision should limit to decide the extraterritorial validity of the marriage and not on the annulment.[173] The court applied the TMICivL of 1940 even when the plaintiff advocated for the application of Argentine law. According to the TMs, claims on annulment should be filed before the judges of the domicile of the spouses and are governed by the law of the place of celebration (Articles 59 and 13 paragraph 1).

II. Divorce

406. Law 2,393 had existed for approximately hundred years, and a reform of the law of marriage was therefore needed. The amendment was accelerated due to jurisprudence. In the case of '*Sejean, Juan B. v. Zacks de Sejean, Ana M.*', the SCJN stated the unconstitutionality of Article 64, Law 2,393.[174] That decision triggered the adoption of Law 23,515, which regulated divorce.

407. Argentine marriage law includes a conflict rule that indicates that 'marital separation and dissolution of marriage are governed by the law of the last domicile of the spouses'. That domicile is where the spouses indisputably had their last effective cohabitation. The localization criterion is followed, which has been welcomed by both doctrine and jurisprudence.[175] This is also the connection that decides the causes and procedure of dissolution, and is only overruled by reasons of international *OP*.[176]

408. There were no regulatory provisions on dissolution until the enactment of that law. *Lex fori* applied to cases in which Argentine judges had to render decisions, and only admitted the death of one spouse as cause of dissolution.

409. Marital separation and divorce result from judicial decisions. Therefore, Argentine law does not recognize effects to agreements that intend to settle marital separation and divorce of spouses domiciled in Argentina.

410. Foreign marriages with a foreign judicial decision establishing a marital separation may be dissolved in Argentina pursuant to the law that applies to those spouses that request such dissolution in Argentina. That request may proceed even in cases in which divorce is not accepted in the state where the marital separation was decided. The only requirement is that one of the spouses domiciled permanently

---

173. SCJN, *Romero López, M. v. D'Auria*, 10 /10/2000, *ED* 192, 233–237, with comment by R.A. Ramayo.
174. SCJN, 27/11/86, *Sejean, Juan B. v. Zacks de Sejean, Ana M.*, *La Ley* 1986-E, 648 with comment by Miguel M. Padilla.
175. Case SCJN, 25/03/60, *Cavura de Vlasov, E. v. Vlasov, A. s. divorcio y separación de bienes*, Fallos 246:87; case SCJN, 09/07/1975, *Jobke, Alfredo J. v. Neidig*, Carlos A.
176. SCBA, 13/06/07, *Behrens, Germán Federico o Hermann Friedrich s/ sucesión ab intestato*, *La Ley online:* AR/JUR/10804/2007.

in Argentina submits before an Argentine judge the foreign decision of martial separation duly legalized.[177]

411. In the new CCC, divorce proceedings must be brought before the judges of the state where the spouses lived together before their separation or, by choice of the actor, before the judges of the domicile or habitual residence of the defendant (Article 2621). In relation to applicable right, the right of the spouses' last domicile shall govern (Article 2626).

III. Legal Effects of Marriage

A. Personal Effects of Marriage

412. Personal relations of spouses were governed, according to the CCC, by the law of the effective domicile of the spouses. To avoid misconceptions, 'effective domicile' was categorically defined as the place where spouses cohabitate. In addition, in the event that domicile was unknown or uncertain, the law of the last place of residence applied.

413. Even when the legislator aimed for certainty, the problem of the mobile conflict is not solved when there is a change in domicile because the law does not indicate at what time the effective domicile must be considered.

414. For the purpose of resolving issues addressing any personal effect of the marriage, the CCC establishes the court attending the case must abide by the provisions laid down by the law of the state where the spouses live together (Article 2624). The connection adopted to regulate the personal effects of marriage maintains the same criterion that inspired Law 23,515, since it did not cause problems at the jurisdictional level or major criticism from the doctrinal stance.

B. Patrimonial Effects of Marriage

415. Autonomous PIL follows a system of unity by not differentiating amongst movables or immovables, protecting materials of strict real character. The connecting factor is the domicile first indicated, and the change of domicile does not alter the law applicable to the patrimonial acts of marriage.

416. The possibility of celebrating marriage conventions was not admitted prior to the enactment of the new CCC. However, conventions celebrated abroad were recognized.[178]

---

177. W. Goldschmidt, *Derecho internacional privado*, 10 ed. updated by A. Perugini Zanetti (Buenos Aires, Abeledo Perrot, 2009), 437.

178. B. Pallares, *Derecho Internacional Privado Matrimonial* (Santa Fe: Rubinzal-Culzoni Editores, 1988), 88; J.C. Capparelli, 'Las Convenciones Matrimoniales en el Artículo 163 del Código Civil. Ley 23,515', *La Ley* 1990-D, 659.

417. It is worth noting that the fact that conventions were not admitted at the internal level made it possible to oppose an *OP* exception to those cases requesting recognition of those celebrated in other countries. This position is founded on the comparative vision generally held by doctrine and jurisprudence, which understands that *OP* is retreating, except for express legal rules. Although *OP* is a necessary principle which cannot be dispensed with, its exceptional character must be respected when it acts to prevent the application of foreign law for matters of indispensable defence of axioms that are absolutely necessary for the order.[179] It is thus not surprising that the new legislation receives the agreement which had already been incorporated into previous projects.

418. Thus in the current CCC, the marriage property regime may be determined by means of conventions celebrated before or after it, and supplementary, in the event of the absence of conventions, the regime established by the law of the first conjugal domicile shall apply.

419. The conventions celebrated prior to marriage shall be governed by the law of the first domicile at which the spouses live together, whereas the conventions celebrated after it shall be regulated by the law of the conjugal domicile at the moment of the celebration. The suppletory property regime that becomes applicable due to the absence of conventions may not affect the imperative Argentine rules referring to issues of a strictly real nature.

420. Regardless of where the marriage celebration was held, the parties may choose to apply Argentine law to their union's property regime, providing this is recorded in a public instrument and does not affect third-party interests (Article 2625).

421. The rule differentiates between the conventions celebrated before the marriage and those celebrated after it. In the first case, a stone system is adopted as an immovable location is assigned – the first conjugal domicile – as a way of ensuring a major protection of the rights of spouses and third parties. When conventions are celebrated after the marriage, the localizing element combines with the temporal factor as the matrimonial convention is governed by the right of the conjugal domicile at the time of its celebration; it therefore also assumes an immutable character for the same purposes.

422. The TMICivL of 1889 indicates that 'prenuptial agreements govern the relationship amongst spouses regarding their property at the time and since the time of celebration, as long as they do not violate the law of the place of location' (Article 40). Even when the Article does not provide the law that governs the substance and form of the prenuptial agreements, being the latter contracts with no established place of performance, the law of the domicile of the spouses applies. The doctrine also understood that those agreements can be ruled by the same law that governs the matrimonial regime when no agreements exist.

179. CNCiv., Sala I, 20/04/1995, *Martoy Samuel s/sucesión ab intestato*, *E.D.*, 162–593.

423. Some changes were introduced with the revision that took place fifty years later (i.e., TMICivL of 1940). The connecting factor was modified by the adoption of the first domicile of the spouses both to matrimonial regimes and to prenuptial agreements. However, this does not apply to all elements of strict real character that are not prohibited by the law of location of property.[180] The TMICivL of 1940 also modifies the limitation of the application of the law to situations of real character preserving the aim of unity of matrimonial regimes.

IV. Spousal Support

424. Domestic law provides rules on the reciprocity of support amongst spouses. Those rules apply to PIL; however, if obligations derive from other juridical family relations, the law applicable to those other relations may apply.

425. Spousal support, both from the perspectives of applicable law and competent jurisdiction, reflected clearly the intention of the legislator to favour the spouse with a credit.

426. The RCC established, with regards to jurisdiction, several options for the filing of claims, since it recognizes competence to: (1) the courts of the marital separation, divorce, or annulment; (2) upon choice of the plaintiff: the judge of the domicile of the spouses; the domicile of the defendant; the judge of the usual residence of the creditor; that of the place of performance of the obligation; the judge of the place of celebration of the support agreement, if the latter is available and if it coincides with the residence of the defendant, if claimed as principal issue (Article 228 RCC).[181]

427. In the new code, Argentine PIL about maintenance obligations has followed existing general guidelines, contained mainly in the RCC and in the CIDIP IV on Support Obligations, systematizing the casuistry in the context of the rule being analysed. Thus the new provision reasserts Argentine PIL tradition, both autonomous and conventional, based on the protection of the weak part of the support obligations.

428. Article 2629 of the CCC lays down that when spouses or common-law-partners are involved, the judges of the last conjugal or cohabitational domicile have concurrent competence, or those of the defendant's habitual residence or domicile or the judge who heard the dissolution of the union.

429. In turn, the right to alimony between spouses or life partners is governed by the law of the last joint domicile, the last effective cohabitation, or the country

180. CNCiv., Sala I, 20/04/1995, *M.S. s/ sucesión ab intestato*, *ED*, 162–593.

181. About the situation for unmarried couples, *see* M.C. Azar, 'Las Obligaciones Alimentarias Internacionales Derivadas de Uniones de Hecho', *Revista de Derecho de Familia y de las Personas*, Año 2 – Número: 2, March 2010, 29–37.

whose law is applicable to the dissolution or nullity of the bond (Article 2630). This involves a divorced couple with two children. The mother lives with them in Argentina while the father lives in Germany. The problem revolves around the alimony payment the children's father is bound to provide, and as there are two different currencies, the problem is also how to make it the payment. So the points are to fix the support payment and determine the currency in which it should be made.

430. The First Instance Court that made the decision under the RCC decided to fix the amount of the maintenance obligations Mr K.M. must pay for his under age children L.S.K.F. and M.K.F. at USD 3,000 per month in advance, establishing it retroactively as from 4 November 2014. The applicant had in turn requested provisional alimony of EUR 500 a month until judgment was passed establishing definite maintenance in favour of both the couple's under-age children. The mother raised an appeal against the judgment, where the Chamber involved ruled in what was undoubtedly a promising usage of the new rules based on the argumentation sustaining the decision.[182]

The collegiate court resolved to accept partially the applicant's appeal, and apply the German law of the alimony debtor's domicile. For this purpose, it highlighted: '... our country is linked to Germany by the Convention on obtaining maintenance obligation abroad, adopted by the United Nations and in force since 1/1/1962'; which was ratified in our country by means of Law 17,156, modified by Law 19,739. The purpose of this convention is to:

> make it possible for a person hereinafter referred to as the plaintiff, located in the territory of one of the contracting parties, to obtain the maintenance obligation he or she claims as a right from another person, hereinafter referred to the defendant, subject to the jurisdiction of another contracting party (Article 1).

The Convention referred to has no rule that applies the *favor alimentari* criterion to determine the governing law. Instead, it establishes that '... the law applicable to the resolution of support obligations proceedings and all the matters emerging from them shall be the law of the defendant's State, including such a State's private international law' (Article 6.3). According to the text of the Convention, then, for purposes of resolving on the maintenance rights of the children regarding their foreign parent, the German legal order is applicable, not because it is the most favourable to the maintenance claim, but because it is the defendant's state.

On the other hand, it also claims that we cannot disregard that when this resolution was made a CCC was in force which contained a whole title (Title IV) on provisions of PIL. In Chapter 3, support obligation is regulated by 'Special Part' in section 4, without distinguishing what link gives rise to the welfare obligation. The new regulations apply a criterion in *favor alimentari* to determine both the jurisdiction (Article 2629) and the applicable law (Article 2630). 'The right to maintenance

182. Cam.1°Apel. Civ., Com., de Paz, Minas, Trib. y Flia. Mendoza. *F., M.C. c/ K., M. p/ Alimentos provisorios– Compulsa*, 19/08/15.

obligation is governed by the right of the creditor's or the debtor's domicile, whichever the competent authority considers the most favourable in the interests of the support obligation of the creditor.'

§5. Parent and Child

I. Child Custody

431. The compliance with rights of a child in PIL has raised several problems in Argentina. The legal doctrine has adopted the term 'custody'. In its legal grounding, it is visible in the rights and duties that derive from parental rights (*patria potestad*) and is referred to as de facto custody. In addition, doctrine and jurisprudence generally refer to 'guardianship,' and de facto custody, and custody are deemed separate terms. Guardianship comprises care, control, and ultimately, the duty of parents to hold and provide for the child.

432. Domestic PIL does not expressly address cases of visitation rights and guardianship when States limit the enjoyment of those rights by the spouses to the national territory and spouses live in different countries. However, that gap has been solved by the Convention on the Rights of the Child that received constitutional hierarchy together with other HRTs.

433. Article 2639 of the new CCC establishes, with regard to Parental Responsibility, that:

> Everything relating to parental responsibility is governed by the law of the child's habitual residence when the conflict begins. Nevertheless, insofar as is required by the higher interest of the child, the law of another State with which the situation is relevantly connected may be taken into consideration.

The law applicable to parental responsibility is governed by the centre of the child's life, but taking his or her higher interest and the principle of proximity as the inspiring criteria. The law of another State with which the situation is relevantly connected may also be considered.

With regard to guardianship and other forms of protection of incompetent persons or those whose competence is restricted, Article 2640 provides that:

> they are governed by the law of the domicile of the person whose protection is being dealt with when the facts determining the guardian occur.
>
> Other institutions for the protection of children and adolescents regularly constituted according to applicable foreign law are recognised and effective in the country, so long as they are compatible with the child's fundamental rights.

434. Also regulated is that in the face of urgent circumstances, the trial judge must apply his or her own law, expeditiously safeguarding the interest to be protected. Regardless of this, the judge is not exempt from fulfilling the obligation laid down by rule making the fact originating the urgent measure known to the Public Ministry or, if applicable, the competent authorities of the domicile or nationality of the person affected (Article 2641). The exception is given by the provisions in relation to the international protection of refugees.[183]

II. International Child Abduction

435. Argentina ratified documents on international child abduction at three levels. First, at a universal level, it ratified the Hague Convention on the Civil Aspects of International Child Abduction. Second, at a continental level, it ratified the Inter-American Convention on International Return of Children, and the Inter-American Convention on Support Obligations (CIDIP IV). Third, at a bilateral level, it ratified a bilateral agreement with Uruguay.

436. As mentioned before, juridical rules are complemented by the universal character of HRTs, yet international child protection suffers fractures which result in the concealment of the aims of the agreements currently applicable. Essentially, and focusing in the efforts to protect the rights of children, it is clearly noticeable of a preoccupation towards solving this problem from the perspective of the child.[184] Regulations intent to cope with the constant changes that result from regular migrations and from the scenario of integration processes that promote free circulation. Harmonization in this field is a difficult task but cannot continue through partial answers because it concerns the global juridical protection of the child.

437. In the CCC, Argentine legislation extends the principles contained in international conventions in force for the Republic in matters of international return of children and all the circumstances that do not belong to the domain of such treaties. Article 2642 establishes that:

> Conventions in force govern in the event of displacement, retention and abduction of children occasioning applications for international finding and return, and outside their area of application, Argentine judges must attempt to adapt the principles of such conventions to the case, ensuring the child's higher interest. The judge with jurisdiction to determine the return of a child must supervise the child's safe return, encouraging solutions tending to voluntary compliance with the ruling. Upon petition of a legitimate party or the requirement of a competent foreign authority, the Argentine judge that learns of the

183. The General Act of Recognition and Protection of the Refugee (No. 26,165) is in force in Argentina, replacing the Executive decree from 1985 (Decree 464/85). Law 26,165 considers a specific procedure to determine whether the status of refugee is granted or denied, the resources available to the person if it is denied, as well as the rights and guarantees throughout the process and once he or she is recognized as a refugee, in ASA, P. and others, *Derechos de Inmigrantes y Refugiados*, en CELS, Informe Anual de Derechos Humanos, (Buenos Aires: Ed. Siglo XXI, 2000), available at www.cels.org.ar.

184. The judgments of the SCJN are dictated in accordance with the protection of the rights of children. *See*: *R., M.A. c/ F., M.B. s/ reintegro de hijo*, SCJN, 22/12/2015, in http://www.csjn.gov.ar/.

imminent entrance into the country of a child or adolescent whose rights might be threatened may establish precautionary measures in order to ensure his or her protection, as well as that of the adult accompanying the child.

438. In this topic, the problem does not evolve around absence of domestic PIL rules or presence of a normative gap.[185] The issue deals with understanding the material scope of application of the convention, the extension given to the reservation clauses, and the interpretation given to the 'best interest of the child'.[186] Thus, in such a wicked scenario as child abduction, it is mandatory to solve the defective interpretation in order to understand the spirit of the international legislator.[187] Even when child abduction is not a new problem, it has increased in alarming proportions. In itself, it is a pandemic of the beginning of the century. However, the constant growth of rates cannot cause surprise given the range of connections and relationships that operate in parallel to the internationalization of the institution of family. Even when this reality does not operate in detriment of the institution of family, an increase in child abduction claims before domestic courts can be noticed.[188]

439. Case law decided in different directions in light of the wording of the international agreements and the interpretation of the conventions ruling child restitution (or not restitution) to the countries where they develop their lives.[189] In this sense, the jurisprudence ruled that restitution should not proceed if fundamental principles are violated (e.g., access to justice arbitrarily denying the possibility of producing evidence).[190]

III. Support Obligations

440. The HRTs and the conventional dimension on child support obligations gain an essential role in Argentina. These provisions are the legal grounding of the institution and reflect the importance of public international law in PIL.[191]

441. All HRTs – in particular the Universal Declaration of Human Rights; the International Covenant on Economic, Social and Cultural Rights; and the Convention on the Rights of the Child – recognize this universal obligation as an

185. *See*: A. Dreyzin de Klor, 'El alcance de la excepción convencional en materia de sustracción internacional de menores: un caso para tener en cuenta', in *Derecho de las Familias, infancia y adolescencia: una mirada crítica y contemporánea*, Graham M. & Herrera M. (Directoras), 1° ed., (Buenos Aires: Infojus, 2014), 157–175.

186. G. Tagle de Ferreyra (dir.), *Interés superior del niño. Visión jurisprudencial y aportes doctrinarios* (Córdoba: Nuevo Enfoque Jurídico, 2009).

187. I. Goicochea, 'Aspectos prácticos de la sustracción internacional de menores', *Jurisprudencia Argentina*, 2006-I; *La Ley* 2006-C, 272.

188. Official statistics have been made available by the Argentine government at www.menores.gov.ar.

189. SCJN, 14/06/95, *Wilner Eduardo Mario v. Osswald María Gabriela*, www.diprargentina.com.ar.

190. SCBA, 15/07/09, *V.M. J. s/ exhorto*, en www.fallos.diprargentina.com.

191. M. Lucero & C. Echegaray de Maussion, 'Alimentos internacionales en el marco de la cooperación internacional', *Actualidad Jurídica-Familia y Minoridad*, N° 68, 7387.

autonomous and individual human right. However, nothing is stated regarding applicable law. Furthermore, Argentina ratified the Inter-American Convention on Support Obligations (Montevideo, 1989) and the Convention on the Recovery Abroad of Maintenance (New York, 1956).

442. Argentina has incorporated a novel rule in its internal legislation, including the maintenance obligations as a fundamental human right. Article 2629 provides that:

> Actions on support obligations, at the choice of the party requesting it, must be brought before the judges of his or her domicile, or habitual residence, or before those of the domicile or habitual residence of the defendant. In addition, if it is reasonable within the circumstances of the case, it can be brought before the judges of the place where the defendant has assets.
>
> Supports actions between spouses or life partners must be brought before the judge of the last conjugal or cohabitational domicile, before the domicile of the defendant's habitual residence, or before the judge who heard the dissolution of the bond.
>
> If an agreement was entered into, at the actor's option, actions may be brought before the judge of the place of performance of the obligation or that of the place where the agreement was entered into if it coincides with the defendant's residence.

443. Protection of the maintenance obligations receiving party is the basic principle guiding the rule of applicable law. Thus Article 2630 regulates that:

> The right to maintenance obligations is governed by the right of the creditor's or the debtor's domicile, whichever the competent authority considers the most favourable in the interests of the party receiving the support obligations.
>
> By choice of the Parties, alimony agreements are governed by the law of the domicile or of the habitual place of residence of either of the parties when entering into the agreement. Failing that, the law governing the right to support obligations is applied.
>
> The right to maintenance obligations between spouses or life partners is governed by the law of the last joint domicile, the last effective cohabitation, or the country whose law is applicable to the dissolution or nullity of the bond.

IV. Filiation

444. The RCC did not include PIL provisions regarding filiation (i.e., the relationship of a child to a parent). Consequently, the gap was solved by the TMICivL 1889 and 1940. The TMICivL of 1940 has the same (and few) provisions as the TMICivL of 1889, and covers an area that is gaining an important dynamic. The American Convention on Human Rights, which has constitutional hierarchy, provides clarity and sustains the duty to recognize 'equal rights for children born out of wedlock and those born in wedlock'.

445. Law 23,264[192] materialized the duty stated in the American Convention on Human Rights and gave strength to the principle of filiation. The law also equalized the effects of filiation in cases of adopted children and children born out of and in wedlock. Notwithstanding, a gap still exists in international jurisdiction[193] and applicable law, and there is a loophole regarding the relationship of filiation through assisted reproduction and subrogation.

446. The TMICivL of 1889 and 1940 grant equal solutions for cases of legitimate filiation and cases of illegitimate filiation that are legitimized as a result of a subsequent marriage. These two situations are governed by the law that regulates the celebration of marriage.

447. The new CCC regulates natural filiation and filiation through AHRT. Article 2631 determines that:

> Actions relating to determining and impugning filiation must be lodged before the judges of the domicile of the party claiming filial location, or before the judges of the domicile of the alleged parent.
>
> For purposes of recognition, the judges of the domicile of the person making the recognition are competent, as well as those of the child's domicile or those of the child's place of birth.

448. Thus the actions received are systematized by means of conflict rules materially oriented to distinguish two categories; the first part of the article regulates 'establishing and impugning filiation', while the last part addresses the 'act of recognizing the child'. This differentiation exists because each of the circumstances presents sufficient entity in its configuration to justify different connections, although all of them are based on safeguarding the same value: *favor filius.*

449. In the matter of applicable law, Article 2632 states that:

> Establishing and impugning filiation is governed by the law of the child's domicile at birth, or by the law of the parent's domicile, or the domicile of the pretended parent at the child's birth, or by the law of the place where the marriage was held, that which offers the most satisfactory solutions for the child's fundamental rights.

450. For the factual circumstance that emerges when the action of recognition of a child born abroad is posed before a national judge, Article 2633 regulates that:

> conditions of recognition are subject to the law of the child's domicile at birth, or at the time of the action, or the law of the author of the recognition's domicile when making the claim. The capacity of the author of the recognition is

192. *BO* 23/10/1985.
193. CNCiv., Sala I, 21/11/2002, *S. B. I. v. C., V. y otro s/ impugnación de maternidad, ED* 201-154.

governed by the law of his or her domicile. The form of recognition is governed by the law of the place of the act or by the law governing it as regards the merits of the case.

With regard to recognition of the filial location constituted abroad, it has also been stipulated that this must be determined in the country pursuant to the principles of Argentine *OP*.

451. Article 2634 also adds that:

> the principles regulating the rules on filiation through assisted human reproduction techniques form part of *ordre public* and must be considered by the competent authority when its intervention is required to recognise the state or registration of the persons born through the use of such techniques. In all cases, the decision best servicing the child's higher interests shall be adopted.

452. From a case law perspective, it is interesting to point out that the Civil Registry of the City of Buenos Aires registered a child born in India from equal co-parenting through a surrogate mother, the first time in which such a registration is performed in the Republic.[194]

V. Adoption

453. With regard to the international regime governing adoption, it is worth noting that Argentina has not signed the 1993 Hague Convention pertaining to Child Protection and Cooperation in Matters of International Adoption. Nor is Argentina party to the bilateral treaties and when the country ratified the Convention of the Rights of Children, it did so in reserve of Article 21, subsections b, c, d, and e.[195]

454. The fundamental purpose of this article is to regulate the duties of the States that recognize or allow the system of adoption, under the perspective of ensuring the higher interest of the child. When our country signed in reserve of this article, it stated that the subsections shall not apply in its jurisdiction under the

194. *D., C. G. y otros c. G.C.B.A. y otros, sobre Amparo (Art. 14 CCABA)*, 22/06/2012 - Expte. 440040.

195. Article 21, subsection (b) states:

> They shall recognise that adoption in another country may be considered ar other means of caring for a child, if he or she cannot be placed in the care of a foster home or delivered to an adopting family, or may not be attended to adequately in his or her country of origin; subsection c) They shall oversee that the child who will be adopted in another country enjoys safeguards and rules equivalent to those relating to adoption in the country of origin; d) They shall adopt all appropriate measures to ensure that, in the event of an adoption in a foreign country, the placement does not give rise to undue financial benefits to those taking part in the process; e) Where appropriate, they shall promote the objectives of this article by concluding bilateral or multilateral arrangements or agreements and shall make every effort within this context to ensure the child's placement in another country is carried out by means of competent authorities or agencies.

understanding that, for them to be applied, a rigorous mechanism must be in place beforehand to protect the child legally from people trafficking and selling in matters of international adoption.[196]

During its eighth period of sessions held in 1994, and after studying and considering the initial report submitted by the Argentine State, The Committee of Children's Rights approved its Final Observations[197] stating its concern regarding the reservations formulated by Argentina to subsections (b), (c), (d), and (e) of Article 21 on account of their scope. Before this decision, the committee recommended considering the possibility of reviewing the reservation with a view to removing it, in view of what was approved in the Declaration and Programme of Action of Vienna.[198] In the session held on 4 October 2002,[199] the Committee approved the final observations to the second periodical report submitted by the country. Said document enjoined the State to make every effort necessary to put to use the recommendations referred to, highlighting in its list of concerns the breaches of the first report.[200]

455. It is worth mentioning that there is a tendency in Argentina towards negatively considering international adoption. This fact is clearly manifested by the national authority.[201]

456. Article 2635 of the new CCC establishes that:

> In the case of children whose domicile is in the Republic, Argentine judges are exclusively competent in deciding on guardianship for adoption and for granting full adoption. Judges from the place which granted the adoption of the adopted party's domicile are competent to override or revoke an adoption.

457. In Argentina, due to the public character of the institution, adoption results from a judicial decision and requires the intervention of the State Office for the Protection of Minors. This dimension is projected to international adoption from a domestic perspective.[202]

---

196. Article 2 conf. Law 23,489 which approves the Convention on Children's Right. O.G. 10/16/1990.
197. www.un.org; CRC/C/15/add.35. (Concluding Observations/Comments).
198. www.un.org/Declaración y Programa de Acción de Viena. In this document, the duty of States to reinforce international and national mechanisms and programmes for the defence and protection of abandoned children, homeless children, those economically and sexually exploited, especially including those used in child pornography and prostitution. Also highlighted is that the full and harmonious development of a child's personality requires him or her to grow up in a family environment.
199. CRC/C/15/Add/187. 9 Oct. 2002.
200. www./CRC/C/15/Add.35 (Concluding Observations/Comments).
201. National Treasury Procurer, MJDDHH, 11/12/2008, *Julio C. Rivera (h) & Laura Huertas s/ solicitud de adopción.* Resolutions 267:526. - Lexis No. 70056575. In that case, the spouses could not adopt in Colombia because Argentina does not allow international adoptions.
202. M.S. Najurieta, 'Coordinación de ordenamientos jurídicos en materia de adopción internacional', (Cordoba: Academia Nacional de Derecho y Ciencias Sociales de Córdoba, 2004).

458. In material for cooperation of parties wishing to adopt abroad, the team collaborated by drawing up the PIL rules for the CCC included in the original text of this article submitted to the RC a paragraph stipulating that:

> the Argentine administrative or jurisdictional authorities must cooperate with people whose domicile or habitual residence is in Argentina, aspiring to an adoption to be granted in a foreign country, applying for social and environmental reports in preparation for or following up an adoption to be granted in a foreign country.

However, this formula has been discarded given the fact that during the draft plan's study stage in the Ministry of Justice, the rule was removed.

459. As to applicable law, the requirements and effects of the adoption shall be governed by the law of the adoptee's domicile when the adoption was granted. In the event of actions overriding or revoking an adoption, these shall be governed by the law of where they were granted or the law of the adoptee's domicile (Article 2636).

460. In addition, to favour the insertion of adoptions constituted abroad – international or simply foreign – within the Republic, it is instituted that an adoption constituted abroad shall be recognized once it has been granted by the judges of the country of the adoptee's domicile when the adoption was granted. Adoptions conferred in the country of the adopting party's domicile must be recognized in the same way as when the adoption can be recognized in the country of the adoptee's domicile (Article 2637).

In this sense, to control the OP, the child's higher interest and the strong bonds of the case with the Republic must be considered.

Chapter 8. Law of Succession

§1. *Lex Successionis*

461. When deciding on applicable law, the systems of unity and fragmentation dispute will govern international successions. On the one hand, the unity of the succession is rooted in the Roman system which adopted these criteria even if the deceased had property in more than one state. Property is regulated by the personal law of the deceased *(Lex patriae* or *lex domicilii*). The roman system is based on the concept of the *pater familiae*; accordingly, the succession implied the substitution of the *pater familiae* by cause of his death. As a consequence, it is organized within the area of family law. On the other hand, the Germanic system considers the institute as a means of acquiring dominion over property of the deceased. Therefore, it is organized within the law of property and the real statute applies as a consequence.

§2. Scope of Application

462. As to the ways of acquiring the dominion, broadly speaking and according to the title and mode, it is considered necessary to have a sufficient deed (enforceable legal act) and a sufficient mode (real legal act) to acquire the real right.[203] Modes may, in turn, be classified as original or derived. According to the former, the acquirer obtains something of his or her own accord, and by virtue of the latter, he or she received it from another. Among the derived modes, it may occur as anticipated inheritance or as actual inheritance, which occurs when the law stipulates that the decedent's rights are transmitted to his or her heirs at the exact moment of his or her death, and the regulation of which must be reconciled with the rules of succession law.

463. Argentina has a system of domestic PIL which establishes that in matters of succession the courts of the decedent's last domicile are competent, with the exception of actions relating to immovables or permanent status assets located in Argentina, in which case national judges assume competence (Article 2643). The new CCC received the thesis accepted by jurisprudence and doctrine.[204]

It also establishes that the law of the decedent's last domicile applies, with the exception of questions related to immovables located in the Republic, in which case Argentine law applies (Article 2644). Thus the new CCC includes an internationally imperative rule for the case of immovables located within the country.

464. On the other hand at the conventional dimension, TMICivL of 1889 and 1940 converge in the most pure system of fragmentation whether in applicable law or jurisdiction. Consequently, the law of the domicile where the goods (movables

203. E.I. Highton, *Dominio y usucapión*, 2da. Parte, (Buenos Aires: Ed. Hammurabi, 1983), pp.1.

204. *See*: CCiv. y Com., Junín, 18/12/14, *Nardi, Juan Carlos s, sucesión, LL* 06/02/15, 7 y en *LL* 2015-A, 206.

and immovables) were located at the moment of death governs all that relates to legitimate and testamentary successions. Therefore, this law will govern the following: form of testaments, capacity to inherit, substantial validity and effects of testaments, titles and rights inherited by the family and surviving spouses, existence and proportion of forced heirship, and existence and amount of goods subject to reserve (Articles 44 and 45, TMICivL 1889 and 1940 respectively). The TMICivL of 1889 also includes the capacity to execute a testament according to *lex situs* (Article 45).

465. However, four exceptions apply to the regime of unity of the succession. First, regarding form, a nuncupative or sealed testament executed through a solemn act will be valid in Member States (Article 44 of both TMs). Second, regarding credits with security, those credits may only be performed in the country where the security is located. Third, the unity of successions applies to testamentary gifts or legacies (Article 49 of both TMs). Finally, the last case relates to collation. Both TMs state that the obligation to collate is governed by the law of the succession to which that property belongs, and when it refers to amounts of money, the latter will be divided proportionally amongst all successions to which the heir owes the collation (Article 50 of both TMs).

§3. Absentees Presumed Dead

466. Argentine legislation in the RCC is silent on provisions of PIL that regulate this area. However, Article 16 Law 14,394[205] refers to jurisdiction.

The gaps are solved by the analogical application of the provisions of the TMICivL of 1940. In the Republic, the courts have jurisdiction if the last domicile or residence of the absentee is located in Argentina (Article 57 of both TMs; and Article 110 RCC). International jurisdiction of Argentine judges will be exclusive in those cases. With the RCC, Argentine judges also have competence if the absentee had property in Argentina. In those cases, the jurisdiction of Argentine courts is concurrent both to that of the foreign judge of the last domicile or residence of the absentee and to that of the judges of other countries in which the absentee owned property.

To come back to the definition a 'vacant inheritance' is alluded to when the decedent has no heirs, either because there are none or because existing heirs waive their rights or are incapacitated from inheriting.[206] In any of these cases, the law governing the succession is to be followed. Actually, the new CCC regulates that if in cases of vacancy the foreign law that is applicable does not attribute succession to the State where the property is located, in any event, any property located in Argentina becomes the property of the Argentine State, either of the Autonomous City of Buenos Aires or the province they are located in (Article 2648).

205. *BO*. 30/07/54.

206. M. Ossorio, *Diccionario de Ciencias Jurídicas, Políticas y Sociales*, (Buenos Aires: Ed. Heliasta,1996), p. 474.

§4. TESTAMENTARY DISPOSITIONS

I. Validity of Testaments

467. Conflict rules regarding testaments present diverse hypotheses.[207] First, the case of a foreigner that executes a testament in a foreign country, yet not in Argentina. Validity of form will be subject to the law of the country where it was drawn up, by the law of the domicile, of the habitual residence, or of the testator's citizenship when drawing up the testament or by Argentine legal forms (Article 2645).

Concerning qualification, the new CCC establishes the principle '*favor testamentii*', which proposes an interpretation always in favour of the validity of the testament.

Also is valid a consular testament, written in a foreign country by an Argentine citizen or a foreigner domiciled at the Argentine state, with the established legal forms of Article 2646.

468. The legislator favours the principle of formal validity of the testament by welcoming the alternative connecting factors, being this the only hypothesis in which nationality is a connecting factor.

469. The capacity to be testator is governed by the law of the domicile of the deceased at the time of the act (Article 2647, CCC).

TMs state that the testamentary requirements must comply with the law of location of the property at the time of death.

II. Interpretation

470. It is paramount to identify the genuine intention of the testator. As to the capacity for leaving a testament, the code follows the general principle of the human person's capacity established in Article 2616, which is why the domicile governs the factual and legal capacity to both grant and revoke a testament.

471. Therefore, the law that the testator aimed for at time of execution must be considered. For this, the rule also incorporates a temporal element – 'at the moment that the act is carried out' – which means that it is indifferent, for the purposes of judging the validity of a testament, whether the decedent was capable or not at the time of his or her death.

Lex situs is also relevant because real rights can be created through testamentary dispositions.

207. I. Weinberg, *Derecho Internacional Privado*, 2da.Ed (Buenos Aires: Lexis Nexis, 2002), 337.

III. Revocation of Testaments

472. According to the CCC, governing law in the State where the decedent is domiciled when the testament is revoked shall determine his or her capacity to perform the act.

Hence it follows that the time factor becomes highly relevant for purposes of determining the validity or not of the act, as the capacity must have existed when revoking the testament, regardless of whether it is later lost.

Part III. Annex: International Civil Procedure

Chapter 1. Sources of International Civil Procedure (ICP)

§1. Introduction

473. The regular foreign traffic can survive if absorbed by law. Hence, provisions generated in international jurisdictions and in the domestic territory are mandatory. Juridical relations with foreign elements can develop and be solved without further obstacles. The latter is possible, thanks to provisions that allow international jurisdiction and a new set of domestic rules focused on international juridical cooperation (IJC), either domestic, conventional or institutional, which allow a better flow of documents. Subsequently, it is no surprise that among thoughts of the contemporary international community a comprehensive expansion of the judicial assistance is observed. The drafting of international agreements facilitates jurisdictional practice by avoiding the forwarding of pleadings, reducing court costs and expenses, and creating bonds amongst countries which deepen their relations.

§2. Domestic Law

474. Legal proceedings concerning civil and commercial matters with foreign law systems are governed by the provisions stated in the AC, HRTs, international treaties, NCCPC, and provincial procedural codes. In addition, the RCC has a number of substantive rules on international jurisdiction which can apply through conflict-of-laws rules. As pointed above, the RCC also has many specific provisions aiming to particular matters (See *supra* Part I, Chapter 1 Sources).

The new CCC provides a regulatory framework on international jurisdiction and international judicial assistance in Articles 2601–2612.

475. Federal laws grant jurisdictional sovereignty to Argentine courts (Articles 75(32) et seq. AC). National jurisdiction is dealt under public law and projects itself in an international level. Its nature reveals that it deals with provisions on international public law, when stating the jurisdiction amongst States. Consequently, is the National Congress (and not the provincial legislatures) which must enact rules regarding when judicial agencies have jurisdiction in claims relating to PIL.

476. Provinces delegated to the federal government the power to rule on substance, retaining for themselves the ability to rule on procedural matters (Article 75(12) AC). Nation and provinces have simultaneous powers regarding compatible issues and that do not fall either under the exclusive competence of the federal government nor are prohibited to the provinces (Articles 125 and 126 AC).

477. The institution of *international jurisdictional cooperation* is ruled now by the new CCC, in the NCCPC (Articles 132, 517, and 519*bis*)[208] and by the provincial procedural codes. Judges will use these provisions in cases of absence of regulations in the conventional dimension (i.e., bilateral or multilateral agreements) or when there are no related agreements in MERCOSUR. As mentioned in the previous chapter, the residual character of PIL is observed.

478. For over a century, the jurisdictional matter also lacks harmonized provisions in domestic PIL (see *supra* General Introduction). There is no organic law that gathers all provisions related either to international jurisdiction or to the system of PIL as a whole (a fact that is even more serious).

479. Consequently, there are many gaps to be covered. The case law and the doctrine propose covering the gaps by using rules with domestic application in the international legal field,[209] or by applying by analogy provisions from international conventions to situations that have no reception because of their scope of application.[210] The SCJN has systematically adopted a third position when using principles that belong to the Argentine system and that are stated in the AC and the HRTs.[211]

480. However, the new CCC has adapted to the new presuppositions of postmodernist PIL, including a chapter on International Jurisdiction, which contains principles of jurisdictional cooperation and international procedural assistance.

481. The sources on this field are interpreted and applied in accordance to the following Human Rights principles (incorporated to the AC):

- Supremacy of international treaties over domestic law.
- Equality of process for foreign citizens.
- Due process.
- Fair and equitable treatment.

208. Law 17,454, NCCPC, modified by Law 22,434, Order 1042/81. The NCCPC has been subject to numerous amendments, being the most recent the one by the Law 25,488 (*BO* 22/11/01).

209. CNacApel., Sala A, 27/11/2009, *Multicanal S.A. v. Grupo Uno S.A. y otros*, *La Ley online*: AR/JUR/58005/2009.

210. Juzg.Esp.Civ.yCom., N° 5, 07/06/77, *Rodríguez, Hugo D. v. Automóvil Club Argentino*, *ED* 77, 269, with comments by W. Goldschmidt; Juz.Nac.Com., N° 7, Secretaría 14, 21/10/86, *Banco do Brasil S.A. v. Astilleros Corrientes S.A.*, www.diprargentina.com; CNCom., Sala E, 13/11/92, *Sasin José Summer v. Casa Dias S.A.C. y otro s.*, www.diprargentina.com.

211. *A., M.S.*, SCJN, 26/3/2008, *DJ* 16/07/2008, *La Ley online*: AR/JUR/1693/2008. In that case, the respect for the 'habitual residence' of the child was followed. The case dealt with competence in a claim on pre-adoptive guardianship in which the best interest of the child was seen as the guiding principle of the Convention on the Rights of the Child and Law 26,061.

– Avoid the denial of justice.

482. International Civil Procedure (ICP) includes mainly provisions on international jurisdiction and on recognition and enforcement of foreign judgments. Beyond these notions, there are other subject matters on international litigation, such as delivery of documents, taking of evidence, and proof and information of foreign law. Some of these issues are included in another area, which is well known as international legal cooperation.

483. The new CCC regulates the equality of treatment in Article 2610 between the citizens and permanent residents abroad, and pointed out that they have free access to justice to defence their rights and interests, under the same circumstances as argentine residents.[212]

The system also considers international jurisdictional cooperation as a duty, where Article 2611 establishes that 'Regardless of the commitments undertaken by international conventions, Argentine judges must provide broad jurisdictional cooperation in civil, commercial, and labour matters.'

484. The factual hypothesis that gives rise to international legal mutual aid occurs when a judge in one State, in proceedings brought before his or her court, needs to request collaboration from a judge in a different State to carry out certain procedural acts in the latter State's territory. Consequently, cooperation is requested to carry out acts such as services, subpoenas, writs of summons or evidence, among others. Thus the purpose is served of not interrupting the continuity of the proceedings brought before one court which, in this aspect, is in the need of requesting assistance from a foreign court.

485. The inclusion of this regulation in the CCC is new to all legal operators, as it acts as a guideline to considerer the IJC as a duty for all States. In addition, as it is expressly regulated in the institutional framework,[213] in the Protocol of jurisdictional cooperation and assistance in civil, commercial labour, administrative, and conventional matters, Las Leñas (Article 1), it covers the vacuum existing in the autonomous regulation in the field, coordinating the levels of regulation under a single principle.

§3. International Conventions

486. International conventions of Argentine PIL in the area of ICP can be classified on different basis. On the one hand, they can be classified according to the

212. C.Nac.Civ., *Eguiguren Laborde, Valeria c. Chiramberro Larrategui, Daniel Carlos s. exequátur y reconocimiento de sentencia extranjera*, Sala L, 18/09/15.

213. C. Lima Marques, 'Procédure civile internationales et MERCOSUR: pour un dialogue des règles universelles et régionales', *Uniform Law Review – Revue de Droit Uniforme NS-Vol. VIII* - 2003-1/2, 465–484.

forum of origin; and on the other hand, they can be classified according to the material scope of legislation.

I. Origin of Sources

487. Part I Chapter 1 mentions conventional and institutional sources and an exhaustive enumeration of treaties ratified by Argentina that relate to the scope in which the rules on ICP developed. Numerous multilateral and bilateral agreements rule on procedural matters. The first of these documents dates to 1889, when the Treaty of Montevideo on International Procedural Law (TMIPL) was adopted, and amended in 1940.

488. The CIDIP and the Hague Conferences have been beneficial to the universe of ICP treaties. Argentina is a Member State to most of those international agreements. In addition, within the framework of MERCOSUR efforts were pursued early to regulate this matter.[214]

489. MERCOSUR provides an important framework for the elaboration of rules on ICP. Amongst the most used instruments are to be mentioned: Protocol on Judicial Cooperation and Assistance in Civil, Commercial, Labour and Administrative Matters (1992) and its Complementary Agreement (1997); Protocol of Provisional Measures (1994) and its Complementary Agreement (1997); and Protocol on International Jurisdiction in Contractual Matters (1994). These protocols currently apply to the four Member States of MERCOSUR.

II. Subject Matters

490. Conventional and institutional agreements have been drafted in the following areas:

- Legalization.
- Powers of attorney to be used abroad.
- Taking evidence.
- Proof of and information on foreign law.
- Exchange of legal information.
- Legal aid.
- Provisional measures.
- Recognition and enforcement of judgment.
- Letters rogatory.
- International jurisdiction.

214. *See*: A. Dreyzin de Klor & T. Saracho Cornet, *Trámites judiciales internacionales* (Buenos Aires: Zavalia, 2005).

Chapter 2. The Principle of *Lex Fori*

491. All issues related to procedure are regulated by the *lex fori* according to procedural rules (NCCPC and provincial procedural codes). The *lex fori regit processum* prevails over the connecting factors related to particular actions or party autonomy, which have no influence on the application of the law of the forum on civil procedure.

492. As a general rule, the law of the country of the court that decides on the case (*lex fori*) will also govern procedure. This solution is applied by all legal systems, even though few expressly proclaim it.[215]

493. In some cases, problems are faced regarding the qualification of situations as pertaining to substance or procedure. The classic example is the extinction of an obligation due to lapsing of a statute of limitation. Common law countries consider the latter a procedural matter or a cause of extinction of the action. Other systems, such as the continental European system, consider it a substantive matter or a temporary limit to the exercise of personal rights.[216] Hence, before determining if an issue relates to a process that is subject to *lex fori*, a qualification of the matter according to Argentine law is needed.

494. The need to first deal with the qualification is broadly recognized. Qualification has been subject to a number of academic discussions. Many problems of qualification can arise. Indeed, one of the main points of debate for scholars is over what has to be qualified, i.e., facts, domestic law rules, or foreign law rules. It can be argued that this is a dispute regarding form rather than substance.

215. A.L. Calvo Caravaca & J. Carrascosa González, *Derecho internacional privado*, Vol. I, 10ª ed., (Granada: Comares, 2009), 512.

216. Peter Hay, Russell J. Weintraub & P. Borchers, *Conflict of Law* (12 ed., Foundation Press-Thomson West, 2004). *See also* Yuval Shany, *Regulating Jurisdictional relations between National and International Courts* (New York: Oxford University Press Inc., 2009).

Chapter 3. International Jurisdiction

§1. General Principles

495. The terms 'jurisdiction' and 'competence' are used indistinctly by legal scholars. However, international jurisdiction technically refers to the power of authorities of a State to decide on a private law case with foreign elements; and refers to the power of foreign authorities to deem recognized and executed a decision in another State. Hence, by drawing territorial limits to the power of courts of one State, jurisdiction is identified with the notion of general competence stated by Bartin,[217] who distinguished between general competence and direct jurisdiction. This concept requires determining if by the application of the jurisdictional rules of a country, the courts of that country have attributions to decide.

496. The right to obtain effective protection from judges and courts is a guiding procedural principle. Furthermore, procedural law exists to provide effective protection of rights and legitimate interests through the judicial system.[218]

497. The predictability of the competent jurisdiction is an informative principle of the system that goes together with the principle of legalization and the abovementioned principle of effective protection from judges and courts. The latter is materialized through access to justice and consequently settles the principle of non-denial of justice granting jurisdiction to Argentine courts even in situations not expressly stated in the law.[219] It is not easy to find limits to the principle of proximity if knowledge of cases is guaranteed by national courts in the event that significant connections exist with the forum.[220]

498. There are provisions that attribute international jurisdiction to foreign authorities (e.g., the hypothesis of negative conflicts of jurisdiction). Accordingly, national judges can assume jurisdiction in exceptional cases, protecting the effective exercise of the right of self-defence and granting access to the jurisdiction. The precedent '*Vlasov*',[221] decided by the SCJN, provides a relevant ruling on this area. The SCJN resolved a matter of international jurisdiction using domestic PIL rules that were included in the Law of Civil Marriage 2,393 (Article 104). The doctrine of non-access to justice used in the domestic jurisdictional framework was applied through analogy of concepts to the international scope, hence avoiding denial of justice.

---

217. E. Bartin, *Études de droit International privé*, 1889.
218. A. Dreyzin de Klor, 'Los instrumentos de cooperación jurisdiccional del Mercosur ¿útiles a la asistencia?', *RDPC* 2009-3, 606.
219. TSNeuquén, 22/06/09, *Kosfelder Stormer, Harry s. sucesión*, *ED* 23/04/10.
220. CNCiv., Sala F, *Zapata Timberlake, Marta M.G. v. Stehlin, Carlos J.F. s/ nulidad de matrimonio*, *ED* 127-602.
221. SCJN, *E. Cavura de Vlasov v. A. Vlasov,* Fallos 246:87; *JA*, 1960-III-216.

499. Every person has the right to due process. This is a constitutional right included in the HRTs and is also the pillar of procedural and substantive processes. The right of self-defence is part of due process.

500. The jurisdiction given to Argentine courts is not deferrable. This provision applies even when international treaties and Law 48 (Article 12 paragraph 4) admit court deferral in favour of foreign judges or arbitrators. Consequently, the requirements of Article 2 NCCPC must be met. That Article reads:

> Court deferral will operate if there is a written agreement by the parties in which they manifestly express their decision to submit the dispute to the agreed jurisdiction. In addition, for petitioners because they submit petitions; and for defendants when answering or opposing to petitions, or when failing to do so without articulating preliminary jurisdictional pleas.

501. Pursuant to Article 2 NCCPC, it is important to determine: (i) when express deferral takes place, and (ii) when tacit submission is admitted. According to Argentine case law, the former must clearly indicate the foreign judge and cannot be deduced from the designation (by the parties) of a certain right to govern a contract. The latter applies to petitioners at time of filling petitions and to defendants at time of filling answers, failing to do so, or opposing exceptions without previous jurisdictional pleas of deferral.[222]

502. Continuing with the enumeration of principles underlying the elaboration of rules on international jurisdiction, it is worth mentioning the principle of effectiveness of decisions. This principle applies to court decisions because it reflects the relation between cases and courts. Through its enforcement, the assumption of competence by national judges is limited because of the possibility of not recognizing the effectiveness of the decisions of local judges in a foreign state.[223]

503. The principle of independence is also essential. It is reflected in decisions of the SCJN that state that it is a principle of *jus gentium* every nation is entitled to because of jurisdiction over 'inhabitants, facts occurring in their territory, and judicial cases resulting from those facts'. However, they do not have jurisdiction over 'facts and cases originated outside of the territory'.[224]

§2. Domestic Rules

504. In order to provide a clear frame of the criteria adopted by the national legislator, it is necessary to comprehend the principles of the basis of jurisdiction. According to this basis, judges support the assumption of competence. Following

---

222. J. Kleimanovich, *Código Procesal Civil y Comercial de la Nación Comentado y Anotado*, Tomo I, 4 ed. Ampliada y actualizada. (Buenos Aires: Abeledo Perrot, 2009), 34–35.
223. CNCiv., Sala I, *Courtenay Luck de van Domselaar, Norah s/ sucesión ab-intestato*, *ED* 162-587.
224. SCJN, *Compte y Cia v. Ibarra y cía.*, Fallos 138:37.

this understanding, a general overview of the principles on which to establish national and international jurisdiction is provided.

I. Types of International Jurisdiction

505. Rules attributing international jurisdiction can be unilateral or multilateral. Unilateral rules are aimed to domestic judges indicating when they have jurisdiction and when they are allowed to know and decide on cases. Multilateral rules establish the country whose judges obtain international jurisdiction on a given subject matter. These rules are not aimed to domestic judges or to their countries, but give judges guidelines to decide on merits of jurisdiction of the requiring authority. The first situation refers to direct jurisdiction, while the second situation refers to indirect jurisdiction.[225]

506. Unilateral rules have a determining function because they provide local judges with duties to act. Multilateral rules mainly deal with values because they only provide to foreign judges (or countries they belong to) expected duties and do not require duties to act. A structural difference is sensed between both rules.[226]

507. Another important difference between the two jurisdictional rules is given by the purpose that inspires them. The rules on direct jurisdiction tend to avoid the effective denial of justice because all cases must have a competent judge. If legislators are national, and by ignoring if foreign countries provide competent judges to the parties, the legislators provide to parties the maximum of opportunities. If legislators are international, they intend to appoint judges that are part of the international community. Indirect jurisdiction, on the contrary, intends to assure the efficiency of certain acts and even of foreign court decisions. Precisely, a condition for the efficiency of foreign court decisions is the compliance with the protection of the international jurisdiction of judges that decided in the cases. At this point, the aim is not to avoid denial of justice, since justice has been already rendered. The purpose is to prevent the improper rendering of justice (e.g., cases in which judges invade the jurisdiction of judges of the country where the efficiency is requested). From this perspective, there is a teleological difference between the rules conferring direct international jurisdiction and the ones conferring indirect international jurisdiction.

II. Nature of Rules That Assign International Jurisdiction

508. Autonomous ICP is, as a general rule, governed by provincial law. This rule needs a more exhaustive explanation when applied to the problematic international jurisdiction. Scholars understood that the Nation had, as a result of its implied

225. J. Fernández Rosas & S. Sánchez Lorenzo, *Derecho internacional privado*, 5 ed. (Madrid, Thomson-Civitas), 82 et seq.

226. W. Goldschmidt,*El S.O.S. en el Derecho Internacional Privado, 35.*

power, a duty to rule on this area and that subsequently the international jurisdictional rules had federal nature because they limited the jurisdictional power of Argentine judges against that of foreign courts.[227] That position is correct, because of the above-mentioned constitutional grounds. The criteria to assign international jurisdiction must be stated by national laws, while the criteria to assign special jurisdiction must continue to be subject to the power of the provinces.

509. Function and nature of jurisdictional rules are different to those of domestic competence. The first limit the power of the state (i.e., the judicial branch considered as a whole). The second distribute amongst the entities of the country the different cases submitted to their jurisdiction according to the rules of international jurisdiction. In this sense, once the nature of the rules assigning international jurisdiction is determined, the following clarifications can be outlined:

(1) Rules assigning international jurisdiction should be present in international agreements unifying the rules to assure the effectiveness at its highest level of cooperation: the recognition and enforcement of foreign judgments, because one of the requirements for international efficiency of foreign judgments is that they proceed from an internationally competent court.
(2) National legislators assume the task when there are no agreements. Hence, those rules assume the role of rules of a federal nature; while provinces preserve the assignment of competence due to territoriality, subject, grade, etc.
(3) Normative gaps can be noticed due to a lack of conventional and federal rules. These gaps are solved by:
   - Analogy with adopted agreements signed by Argentina.
   - Application of principles of extension to domestic territorial competence rules, with the necessary adaptation due to the international character of the controversy.[228] While adopting this criterion, it is necessary to gain a common and coordinated parameter which will be a reference for domestic procedural legislation of the provinces, in order to obtain harmonized results. Otherwise, *forum shopping*[229] amongst provinces could be possible due to the ability to elect the criteria to attribute provincial competence. This election, applied by extension, leads to choosing the most favourable applicable law to the pretentions of plaintiffs. The principle of official character applies according to reasons of *OP*, even when parties can claim them. The legal doctrine of the SCJN is very useful in providing harmonization to this matter.[230]

---

227. M.A. Gelli, *Constitución de la Nación Argentina Comentada y Concordada*, 2ª ed. (Buenos Aires: La Ley), 560–563.
228. S. Palacio de Caeiro, *Competencia federal civil-penal* (Buenos Aires: Edit. La Ley, 1999), 46 et seq.; R. Haro, *La competencia federal. Doctrina, Legislación y Jurisprudencia* (Buenos Aires: Edit. Depalma, 1989), 75.
229. Juzg.Nac.Com., N° 13, Secretaría 26, 12/04/76, *Ocerín, José Pascual v. Talleres Auxiliares de la Industria Minera S.A. (TAIM S.A.)*.
230. SCJN, 24/02/09, *Compañía General de Negocios pide la quiebra Mihanovich, Ricardo L.*, CNCom., Sala C, 27/04/10, *RDCO* 237, 155–167, with comments by A.Dreyzin, 'La CSJN ubica cada ficha en su casillero', *DeCITA*, 11.2009, Insolvencia Internacional (Paraguay: CEDEP), 200–246.

510. In another line of thought, international jurisdiction of courts has traditionally raised less academic interest than choice of law. However, case law increasingly reflects the importance of international jurisdictional issues, as evidenced by the growing number of decisions of lower and upper courts that deal with the issue.[231]

511. Jurisprudence has done its best to explain that direct jurisdiction rules (i.e., jurisdiction analysed by the judges in order to know if they have jurisdiction to make a decision on the claim) tend to avoid effective denial of justice.[232] No litigation can stand without competent judge. If legislators are national, and by ignoring if foreign countries provide competent judges to the parties, the legislators provide to parties the maximum of opportunities. If legislators are international, they intend to appoint judges that are part of the international community.

III. Forums Establishing Jurisdiction

A. Exclusive Forums

512. Exclusive forums find grounding in the specificity of the subject of the judicial matter, and in the strong connection between litigation and country that turn them exclusive. Argentine courts are the only ones who can intervene in those cases to the extent that competence of foreign courts is unacceptable because national legislators have decided in that sense.[233]

513. According to the law, exclusive forums derive mainly from the respect to the 'principle of sovereignty'. They govern in cases on immovables located in Argentina[234] or respond to OP reasons.[235] Pursuant to rules of police (public policy), the national legislator opted for the *lex fori* as applicable law to international cases, inspired in general and public interests of the country involved. Regarding international jurisdiction, *lex fori* requires the intervention of Argentine judges. Motivated by the above mentioned, judges apply the law of their countries when choosing applicable law. A parallelism can be drawn between rules of police and domestic international jurisdiction with an exclusive character.

---

231. L. Usunier, *Regulating the Jurisdiction of Courts in International Litigation: Towards a Global Answer in Civil and Commercial Matters* vol. IX, 541–542 (A. Bonomi & P. Volken eds, *Yearbook of Private International Law* (European Law Publishers/Staempfli Publishers Ltd. Berne, 2007).
232. *Vlasov*, SCJN, Fallos 246:87; *Jobke, Alfredo J. v. Neidig*, Carlos A., CSJN, Fallos 291:540 y *Compte y Cía.v. Ibarra y Cía.*, SCJN, 16/11/36, Fallos: 317:868.
233. SCBA, 13/06/07, *Behrens, Germán Federico o Hermann Friedrich s/ sucesión ab intestato.*
234. Article10 RCC.
235. Another example is provided in the cases of absentees and absentees that are presumed dead, in which the judge of the last domicile in Argentina of that who is presumed dead has exclusive international jurisdiction (Art. 110 RCC). Also, exclusive international jurisdiction will fall on Argentine courts in cases of total or partial charter, or transportation of general goods with the obligation of delivering the goods in Argentina (Art. 614 Law 20,094). *See* P. All, 'Las normas de jurisdicción internacional en el sistema argentino de fuente interna', in *DeCITA* 4.2005, Litigio Judicial Internacional (Buenos Aires: Zavalía, 2005), 422.

514. The new CCC receives the exclusive jurisdiction in Article 2609, which establishes that:

> *Regardless of the stipulations in special laws, Argentine judges have exclusive competence in the following cases:*
>
> *a) in the field of real rights over property located in the Republic;*
> *b) in the field of the validity or nullity of registrations made in Argentine public registries;*
> *c) in the field of registrations or validity of patents, trademarks, designs or drawings and industrial models, and remaining analogous rights in filing or registration, when the filing or registration has been requested or carried out or completed in Argentina.*

The exclusive forums are grounded on the specialization of the issue this judicial matter addresses and the strong link between litigation and the country making them exclusive. These are cases in which the Argentine court is the only one that can intervene, to the extent that competence of a foreign court is unacceptable in our country, as national legislators have determined it thus based on *OP*, on internationally imperative norms and on the public interest.

Indeed, with the aim of preserving national sovereignty and public faith, only Argentine judges may make valid and enforceable rulings in matters related to real rights over real property located in Argentina, declarations of validity or nullity of registry entries and as regards intellectual property rights.

B. Unique Forums

515. Unique forums differ from exclusive forums because, even when a single forum is established, unique forums are not inspired by reasons of international OP, yet they deal with practice.

516. Indeed, the jurisdiction is *unique* when, for practical reasons, it is centralized in a single State taking into account a particular factual aspect (e.g., the last domicile of the deceased as a criterion for attributing competence for initiating succession proceedings, thus avoiding the complexity involved in selecting a different forum).

This example was given by the RCC, when stating that the only jurisdiction that could apply in situations of Article 3284 would be that of the last domicile of the deceased.[236]

236. Article 3284 RCC:

> Jurisdiction and venue over the succession pertains to the courts of the last domicile of the decedent. The following actions must be filed therein: 1. Suits concerning hereditary property, up to and including partition, when they are brought by some of the universal successors against their

517. Article 2643 of the new CCC determines that in matters of succession, the courts of the last domicile of the decedent are competent, with the exception of actions related to real property located in Argentina, in which case national judges assume competence. Thus unity is established concerning the jurisdiction of successions.

C. Simultaneous Forums

518. Simultaneous forums apply when rules grant jurisdiction alternatively to two or more countries.

519. In the RCC, Articles 1215 and 1216 were examples of simultaneous forums.[237] This alternation is justified by giving plaintiffs the possibility to file actions before judges of different countries if there are reasonable connections or connections derived from party autonomy.[238]

520. According to Article 2621 of the CCC, any action related to the validity, nullity or dissolution of the matrimonial institution, or its personal effects or assets, must be brought before the judges of the State where the spouses lived together before their separation or, by choice of the actor, before the judges of the domicile or habitual residence of the defendant. It is an option inherited from Act 23,515, which is broadly accepted in the Republic in terms of doctrine and jurisprudence, to which habitual place of residence is added as the connection point.

521. The new CCC also incorporates an example of simultaneous forums in Article 2629 on support obligations. Given the protection required by the creditor in this institute, the jurisdiction is concurrent among numerous forums, and the options prioritize the interests of the weaker party within the relationship. If it is reasonable within the circumstances of the case, he or she may lodge proceedings before the judges of the State in which the defendant owns assets (assets forum). When spouses or common-law-partners are involved, the judges of the last conjugal or cohabitational domicile have concurrent competence, or those of the defendant's habitual residence or domicile or the judge who heard the dissolution of the union. If an agreement was made, the judges of the place of performance of the obligation or of the place where the agreement was entered into are competent, as long as it coincides with the defendant's domicile.

---

co-heirs. 2. Suits relating to warranty of the shares among co-heirs, and those seeking the reformation or nullity of partition (division). 3. Suits relating to the execution of the dispositions of the testament, even if by particular title, as those relating to the delivery of legacies. 4. Personal actions of the creditors of the decedent prior to the division of the inheritance.

237. Article 1215 RCC: 'In all contracts that must be performed in the Republic, the debtor may be sued in Argentine courts, even if the debtor were not domiciled in Argentina or resided thererin'.

238. *See*: B. Kaller de Orchansky, *Nuevo Manual de Derecho Internacional Privado* (Buenos Aires: Plus Ultra, 1990), 453.

522. Another example reflected in Article 2631 of the CCC which, for actions related to establishing or displacing *status filii*, provides that when determining of impugning filiation by natural means or through AHRT, the actor may choose between the courts of his or her domicile or of the other parent's domicile, while in actions recognizing filiations constituted abroad, the alternative is between the judges of the actor's domicile, those of the child's domicile, or those of the child's place of birth. Accordingly, the solutions proposed in matters of filiation through natural means or AHRT, they follow the trend based on the forum most favourable to the establishment of the bond.

D. General Forums

523. The examples that follow are of general forums that grant jurisdiction to Argentine judges regardless of the subject matter of the affected PIL. That is to say that they are *general forums,* which attribute competence to the judges of one State, whatever the matter involved, based on general criteria which link the case to national judges. They are forums that take an element existing in all the cases as the criterion to determine jurisdiction.

524. Argentine judges shall have jurisdiction when defendants are domiciled in the Republic. This forum prevails in Argentina for cases on international breach of contracts[239] due to the advantages it provides to both parties. Plaintiffs are beneficiated because, if prevailing in their claims, goods existing in the territory will be available for their credits. Defendants are beneficiated because they may litigate before the judges of their own domiciles.

525. Article 2608 of the CCC establishes *'The domicile or habitual place of residence of the defendant. Except for a particular provision, personal actions shall be lodged before the judge of the domicile or habitual place of residence of the defendant.'*

526. The forum of the domicile, made up of corpus and animus (centre of life and the will to reside there), is generally highly relevant in the Argentine system of international jurisdiction as a number of institutions authorize it as the only or concurrent internationally competent forum. Domicile forum is extremely relevant in the Argentine system of international jurisdiction because a considerable number of institutions welcome domicile as a unique or alternative international jurisdiction.

527. The forum of habitual place of residence, in turn, is also widely used; it comes mainly from international sources which adopt it in conventions, especially in the more modern, referring to the place where the centre of life (corpus) is, without requiring animus as determined by configuration of the domicile.

239. Article 1215 RCC.

528. The domicile and habitual place of residence enjoy considerable acceptance as general forums because they enforce the principle of equality provided for in the reform of autonomous PIL and answer to the principle of actual proximity.

529. Another example of general forum is when parties opt for jurisdiction. That is to say, *prorrogatio fori* for cases expressly admitted pursuant to Article 1 NCCPC.

530. The extension of the jurisdiction, as a derivation of the principle of autonomy of will, is currently received by the new CCC in the Article that establishes 'Agreement on the choice of forum. In the matter of assets and international issues, the parties are authorised to extend the jurisdiction to judges or arbiters outside the Republic, except when Argentine judges enjoy exclusive jurisdiction or the extension is forbidden by law.'

In this regard, the drafting of Article 2605 raises the matter to a federal level and grants a solution that harmonizes the criterion throughout the Argentine territory.

531. Thus Article 2606 establishes 'Exclusive character to the choice of forum. The judge chosen by the parties enjoys exclusive competence, unless they expressly decide otherwise.'

532. It is thus consistent that the judge to whom competence is extended by virtue of an agreement of the parties and within the limits laid down by Article 2605, should understand in the matter raised to the exclusion of judges from other States, unless the parties have decided otherwise.

533. The relevance of this provision, also new in the Argentine system of autonomous PIL, is to reinforce certainty on the international jurisdiction, since it settles any doubts regarding concurrence of forums when the parties remain silent.

534. In keeping with the dispositions of the NCCPC (Article 2), the new CCC incorporates Article 2607 on:

> Express or tacit extension. Extending the jurisdiction is operational if it emerges from a written agreement whereby the interested parties express their decision to submit to the competence of the judge or arbiter before whom they appear. Any means of communication which enables evidence to be established by means of a text is also admitted. For the actor, the extension also operates from the fact of having lodged the suit and, with regard to the defendant, of having answered it, fails to answer it, or files prior exceptions without raising a plea.

535. This provision of a federal nature is thus currently tuned into the procedural legislation which has been covered by important jurisprudence with according to the forms in which this prerogative available to the parties operates.[240]

240. J.L. Kielmanovich, *Código Procesal Civil y Comercial de la Nación. Comentado y anotado*, T. I, 4th edition. (Buenos Aires: Abeledo Perrot, 2009, 35).

536. International patrimonial forum grants international jurisdiction to judges of the countries where the patrimony of the defendants is located. If patrimony is constituted by credits, the latter are considered located at the domicile of the debtors. If the action implies restitution of a thing, the patrimony that determines jurisdiction will be that where the things are located.

537. This forum is welcomed by domestic PIL. For example, the new CCC admits this forum subsidiary if the absentee has goods in the Republic in Article 81. In these cases, national judges have jurisdiction even when absentees did not have in Argentina neither the last domicile.

In addition, Law 24,522 allows filing for bankruptcy in Argentina when goods are located there and when the debtor is foreigner (Article 2 paragraph 2).

538. Emphasis is given to the place where damages occur, where interests are located, or where rights are violated. Therefore, the forum of the place where effects of obligations occur applies to tort cases. In an Argentine decision,[241] and following the scope of the petition, the forum was triggered for the collection of a compensation for damages originated due to the breach by a licensor of a *know-how* contract on the commercialization of a licence of a brand based on an instrument that the plaintiff considered a preparatory or preliminary contract. In this case, an extensive interpretation of 'place of performance' was made, sustaining that according to the scope of the RCC (Articles 1215 and 1216) the place of performance was that where the effects of the breached obligations were located and from which the object of the claim derived. This case is an important precedent of the new rule.

539. Article 2650 of the new CCC states that 'Where there is no valid agreement regarding the choice of forum, the following are competent in understanding the actions resulting from a contract, at the actor's choice: (…) b) the judges of the place of performance of any of the contractual obligations … '

540. Indeed, in order to facilitate the interpretation, it is established that the place of performance of any of the contractual obligations is viable for enabling the forum. This precludes all confusion resulting from interpreting the 'place of performance' on the one hand, and clarifies the scope allocated to the connection by using the plural term 'obligations' on the other.

E. *Special Forums*

541. Special forums determine which domestic court of the country with international jurisdiction will decide on a case according to their own jurisdictional rules.

542. Parallelism as an attributive criterion of jurisdiction implies competence of judges of the country whose laws apply to the substance of the process. This principle is not considered of exclusive competence because it would imply the denial

241. CNCom., Sala A, *Benettar SAIC v. Benetton S.P.A.*, 30/5/91.

of extraterritoriality of foreign law. This applies in Argentina to cases falling under the scope of the TMs of 1889 and 1940. Accordingly, Article 56, first part, of those treaties reads:

> Personal actions shall be submitted before judges of the place of the law that governs the juridical acts that motivate the litigations.

543. This criterion is recognized by convenient and practical foundations because judges of the place which laws are applicable are the ones with better knowledge of those laws. Also, problems such as qualification, *renvoi*, and international *OP* could be avoided.

IV. Immunity from Jurisdiction

544. Immunity from jurisdiction is a principle stated by the Argentine law (Law 24,488) and jurisprudence.[242] It cannot be neglected because it is considered a public policy principle of Argentine law. The requirement mentioned in the NCCPC (Article 517, paragraph 4)[243] may not be neglected either.

Article 1 of this law establishes that *'Foreign States are immune to the jurisdiction of Argentine courts, in the terms and conditions laid down by this law.'*

545. Article 2 provides that:

> *Foreign States may not invoke immunity of jurisdiction in the following cases:*
>
> *a) When they consent expressly through an international treaty, a written contract or a declaration in a particular case, that Argentine courts exercise jurisdiction over them.*
> *b) When it is the subject of a counterclaim directly linked to the main claim brought by the foreign State.*
> *c) When the lawsuit deals with a commercial or industrial activity carried out by the foreign State and the jurisdiction of the Argentine courts results from the contract invoked or from international law.*
> *d) When they are sued for labour issues by Argentine nationals or residents in the country, derived from contracts entered into in the Argentine Republic or abroad with effects in the national territory.*
> *e) When they are sued for losses and damages derived from crimes or quasi-delict (negligence) committed in the territory.*
> *f) When it deals with actions on real estate that immovables within the national territory.*

242. JNContAdmFed., N° 9, 02/03/2010, *Claren Corporation v. EN – (Arts 517/518 CPCC Exaquatur) s/varios*, *EL Dial*, 2010. CNCyC, Sala F, Sala III, 22/11/05, *Overseas Union Insurance Limited*, pub. Lexis N° 35003817.

243. SCJN, 22/12/94, *Manauta, Juan J. y otros v. Embajada de la Federación Rusa*, Fallos: 317:1880, *LL* 1995-D, 21.

g) When it deals with actions based on the quality of the foreign State as heir or legatee of assets that are located outside the national territory.
h) When, there being a written agreement to submit all litigation related to a commercial transaction to arbitration, immunity of jurisdiction of Argentine courts is pretended in proceedings related to the validity of the interpretation of arbitration proceedings or with reference to the reversal of an arbitral award, unless the arbitral agreement should provide otherwise.

546. Immunity from jurisdiction consists of the rights recognized to each state (due to their sovereignty) of not being subject to the jurisdiction of another state. It is based on the principles of sovereignty, equality, and independence which are contained in the rule *par in parem non habet imperium.*[244] This immunity protects States before government or sovereign acts unless jurisdiction was expressly deferred.[245] A case decided by the SCJN[246] considered that an act of deferment of the payment of a debt[247] implied an expression of national sovereignty beyond the terms proclaimed to foreign creditors.

547. In another case resolved by the SCJN, the Attorney General ruled:

> that, in the case of court orders, the issuance of phytosanitary certificates by the British authorities within the context of an international sale and purchase, may not be classified as an act of iure gestionis, according to the doctrine of the court delivering judgement: 321:2594 (Whereas 13 of the majority vote). Indeed, it is my understanding that this is an activity reflects the exercise of imperium by the State and, therefore, is comprised in article 10 of Law 24,488 of Jurisdictional Immunity of Foreign States before Argentine Courts, such that for a foreign court to verify examination of the acts of a sovereign State and perchance declare it invalid by means of a ruling against the will of the latter would no doubt endanger the relations between governments and disturb the peace of nations (Fallos: 178:173; 323:3386, among others, and ruling by the Attorney General published in Fallos: 330:5237).[248]

---

244. A. Dreyzin de Klor, 'Comparecencia de un Estado extranjero ante los Tribunales argentinos', *Revista La Ley*, Buenos Aires, 1995; M. Hertz, 'La Nueva Convención de UN sobre Inmunidad de Jurisdicción de los Estados y sus bienes, Su compatibilidad con el régimen argentino', *ED* 215, 929.
245. CNCyCFed., 3/9/98 in re*García Mario Enrique v. Embajada de la República Islámica de Paquistán, ED* 181-391.
246. SCJN, *Brunicardi*, Fallos 319:2886. The SCJN confirmed the existence of a principle of law of nations 'that make it possible to exempt the State from international responsibility for suspending or modifying all or part of the service of the foreign debt in the event that it is forced to do so for reasons of urgent financial necessity' (whereas 16).
247. Sobre los fondos buitres véase: A. Dreyzin de Klor & I. Ellerman, *Los fondos buitres en la plataforma internacional* (Santa Fe: Rubinzal Culzoni ed., 2014).
248. SCJN, 10/06/2014, *Louge A. Beltrán y otro el Gobierno de su Majestad Británica - Daños y Perjuicios*.

Chapter 4. Recognition and Enforcement of Foreign Judgments

§1. EXEQUATUR

548. Exequatur means the permission to enforce a judgment delivered in one state in another state. This possibility is performed through a legal procedure in the state where the permission is required (state of enforcement). The court in the state of recognition and enforcement must determine if the judgment can be enforced domestically disregarding the merits of the claim.[249]

549. An exequatur procedure is required for the enforcement of a judgment in another state. Exequatur has been correctly determined as an expression of sovereignty because a plaintiff who intends to enforce a judgment against property of a defendant in another state must initiate new proceedings in the state of enforcement. The order of the court to enforce a judgment will be deemed an internal order of the state of enforcement.

550. The NCCPC dedicates a chapter to foreign decisions and arbitration awards from foreign tribunals.[250] However, the new CCC deliberately excludes provisions on the rules of recognition and enforcement of foreign judgments.

551. As a general rule, decisions from foreign courts will be enforceable according to the dispositions of international treaties that connect Argentina with the States of origin of the decisions. If there are no connecting treaties between the countries of origin and Argentina, the following requirements must be met:

- The foreign decision must be a final judgment in the state where it was rendered.
- The decision must be rendered by a competent court pursuant to the Argentine provisions on international jurisdiction.
- The decision must result from personal actions or real actions on movables.
- That the defendant be personally subpoenaed and be granted legitimate defence.
- That the decision complies with foreign requirements on validity and with requirements of authenticity pursuant to Argentine law.
- That the decision does not conflict with an Argentine decision, either previous or contemporaneous.
- That the decision does not affect principles of Argentine *OP*.

552. To comply with the requirements of recognition of foreign decisions and arbitration awards, interested parties must submit before lower courts in Argentina legalized and translated copies of the decisions. In addition, parties must submit proof of having enforced the judgments, together with proof of compliance of all

249. *See*: P. van der Grinten, *Abolishing Exequatur in the European Union: An Alternative* 72 (P. van der Grinten & T. Heukels ed., *Crossing Borders Essays in European and Private International Law, Nationality Law and Islamic Law in Honour of Frans van der Velden*, Deventer: Kluwer Law, 2006).

250. Book II, Title I, Ch. II. I., NCCPC.

other requirements if the latter are not contained in the decisions. If the enforcement of foreign decisions proceeds, it will follow the same procedure as that followed by decisions rendered by Argentine courts.[251]

553. When the authority of a foreign decision is claimed in Argentina, it will 'only be effective' if it complies with the above-mentioned requirements.[252]

§2. International Judicial cooperation

554. International judicial cooperation is a part of PIL in general, and a part of ICP in particular. Jurisdictional cooperation occurs when a judge from a state where a process is being developed requires collaboration from a foreign judge to fulfil certain foreign procedural acts, which will eventually be incorporated to the local process.

555. There are three degrees of requested collaboration. Those degrees are motivated, because the degree of assistance will match with the requirements that must be complied in order to render the assistance. Those degrees will depend on the effects that the requested procedure produces in the foreign state.

556. The first degree encompasses the collaboration through simple procedural acts (e.g., notifications, summons, subpoenas), taking of evidence, and information on foreign law. The second degree encompasses precautionary measures. The third degree encompasses the recognition and enforcement of foreign judgments and is considered the most complete judicial cooperation. The *OP* filter covers all levels of cooperation.

557. The collaboration implies the surrender of the ability to render a decision by allowing the effects of a foreign authority to have impact on the local forum. Therefore, it does not only deal with the collaboration with an activity to be performed abroad or closely related to a foreign state. Currently, it has even achieved independence from international judicial cooperation and has its own identity due to the importance it has within the scope of PIL. Recognition and enforcement of judgments and arbitral awards has become independent of cooperation after acquiring its own entity; it has become one of the three pillars of current PIL. Recognition standards are of a federal nature as Argentine doctrine and jurisprudence has recognized.

558. However, the new CCC regulates the international procedural assistance of first degree in Article 2612.[253] This Article establishes:

---

251. According to Art. 518 NCCPC.
252. According to Art. 519 NCCPC.
253. *See*: A. Dreyzin de Klor, 'Title IV. Disposiciones de Derecho Internacional Privado', in *Código Civil y Comercial de la Nación Comentado,* Tome XI, R.L. Lorenzetti (dir.), (Santa Fe: Rubinzal Culzoni ed., 2014), 473–675.

Regardless of the obligations undertaken in international conventions, communication addressed to foreign authorities must be made through letter rogatory. When required by the situation, Argentine judges are authorised to establish direct judicial communications with foreign judges who accept the practice, insofar as due process guarantees are respected.

(p3) Measures that constitute a mere formality and evidence requested by foreign jurisdictional authorities must be complied with so long as the resolution ordering them does not affect principles of ordre public in Argentine law. Letters rogatory must be arranged ex officio and without delay, in accordance with Argentine laws, irrespective of establishing what is pertinent to the expenses demanded by the assistance required.

559. In the last part of the rule, the CCC makes reference to the principles that govern IJC, laying down the fundamental guidelines:

(a) *Instigate proceedings* ex officio: when the rule mentions that letters rogatory must be arranged ex officio and without delay, it refers to the fact that once the judge has received the request for cooperation, there is no need for either party to instigate proceedings to carry out the proceedings required for the measure applied for to be enforced.
(b) *Gratuitous*: on the whole, the act of cooperation is gratuitous. Nevertheless, there may be cases in which there in no gratuitousness, for example, if cooperation is requested for evidentiary measures, the cooperation is gratuitous, but executing the evidence generates expenses that must be covered by the requesting party.

I. Modes of Cooperation

560. It must be first stated that the collaboration is performed through jurisdictional or extra jurisdictional letters rogatory. The former are undertaken by government diplomats or by the interested parties. The latter are undertaken by members of administrative or judiciary offices (e.g., central authorities appointed by the state).

561. Authorities in Argentina are administration officers and their existence is recognized in bilateral and multilateral conventions, both in the regional and universal level. Those authorities do not replace judicial authorities, and their main activity is to execute letters rogatory. Therefore, they bridge foreign judicial authorities, to provide continuity in the process by avoiding the delays or interruptions that national boundaries may generate. In Argentina, the central authority that provides that assistance is the General Office of Juridical Affairs of the Ministry of Foreign Affairs, International Trade and Cult (MFAITC).

II. Domestic Law

562. The NCCPC regulates the assistance that foreign judicial authorities provide and request. Articles 5 and 6 provide general and special rules on competence of Argentine courts. According to those articles, civil and commercial matters include, amongst others: personal actions; real actions on movables and immovables; personal actions that derive from delicts and quasi-delicts; actions that relate to rendering of accounts; actions that relate to the collection of taxes, duties, or fines; actions of marital separation, divorce, nullity, and effects of marriage; the processes of declaration of incapacity due to insanity or deaf and dumb; the requests of additional copy or rectification of errors in a public document; the legalization of testaments; the actions that derive from relations of companies; and claims for the collection of common expenses that apply to immovables subject to condominium.

563. Argentine procedural law applies as subsidiary to other areas of law. The latter, even when they contain their autonomous and adjective regulations, have expressly stated that the NCCPC applies to what has not been ruled, as long as it is not incompatible (e.g., Argentine Law on Labour Procedure[254] and the 'Law on Solidarity of Social Welfare').[255]

564. Communications to and from foreign judicial authorities only proceed by letter rogatory (Article 132 NCCPC). This requirement differs from the criteria followed by some international conventions that welcome a broader scope.[256]

565. Argentine law does not indicate expressly those legitimized to deliver letters rogatory. However, judicial practice reflects that request from foreign judges are presented before the MFAITC, which then delivers the letters to the MJHR. The latter, delivers the letters to local judges with jurisdiction according to local laws of distribution of competence. Once the requests of assistance included in the letters are complied with, they are returned through the same process. When local authorities require assistance from foreign courts, once formal requirements are fulfilled, letters rogatory must be delivered to the MFAITC for legalization.

566. The rule of procedure states that 'the same requirements established in the international treaties and agreements, and the rules of superintendence',[257] shall

254. Law 18,345, Resolution N° 106/98 (*BO* 30/1/98), Title V, Application of the NCCPC. Art. 155: (Applicable dispositions). The following dispositions will apply, as long as they do not conflict with this law: […] Art. 132. All other dispositions of the NCCPC are subsidiary as long as they are compatible with the procedure established in this law.

255. Law 24,463 (*BO* 30/3/95), Ch. 2: Reforms in Judicial procedure and Social Welfare. Article 15: The resolutions of the National Administration of Social Welfare may be challenged […] by means of self-sufficient petitions that will be resolved according to the rules of summary proceedings included in the NCCPC and amendments included in that law.

256. Article 2, CIDIP I on Letters Rogatory, enables requests from 'jurisdictional offices' of Member States. Article 6, Protocol of Las Leñas, follows these same criteria when dealing with the contents of letters rogatory: '[…] a) name and domicile of the jurisdictional office that requires the letter rogatory … '.

257. *See* the Rules on National Justice, Court Resolution of 17/12/52, SCJN, Current text available at Boletín Informativo N° 33, *Anales de Legislación Argentina, LL*, 1998, 1-38. *See* especially Art. 124, which deals with legalization of signatures of judges and officials that intervene in the proceedings.

apply. Therefore, a 'delivery' to conventional law takes place, which even when not expressly indicated, binds related States.

567. The requisites of these instruments may result from different sources (conventional, institutional or internal) and, although they vary depending on the subject matter of the cooperation, broadly speaking all letters rogatory must comply with three groups of requirements:

(a) *Formal*: to ensure the authenticity, understanding and correct application of the measures. Examples of formal requirements are legal copies and translations of the documents drafted in another language.
(b) *Procedural*: to ensure due process guarantees and the best protection of the interests of the affected party. For example, offering counter measures in cases where preventive measures are applied for.
(c) *Substantial*: These ensure respect for the non-derogable values of the requested State, whereby this group of requirements relates to proving that the letter rogatory and the measure requested therein do not violate the *OP*.

568. Argentine authorities may examine if formal requirements of letters rogatory from foreign judges are met.[258]

569. According to Argentine law, parties must provide translations into Spanish of all documents presented in another language before Argentine government divisions, and public, judicial, and administrative offices. Those translations must be completed by certified translators from the country of origin.[259] The jurisprudence has stated that this requirement relates to the liability of translators because their role resembles that of expert witnesses.[260]

570. Article 132 NCCPC includes two cases in which letters rogatory might not proceed. First, when the authorities that require the letters have no competence according to Argentine rules of international jurisdiction. Second, when the resolutions that instruct the letters violate Argentine *OP*.

571. Jurisdictional control by Argentine courts is not justified when dealing with simple procedural acts because cooperation is favoured. In this respect, Article 2611 of the CCC referred to above is new to all legal operators, as it acts as a guideline to considerer IJC as a duty for all States.

572. The applicable national jurisdiction will be fully secured by a request of recognition and enforcement of the judgment rendered in the process that motivated the request of assistance. The simple eventuality does not legitimize the denial of assistance. The jurisprudence decided in those same lines when stating that: 'International competence must be requested before the requiring judge or eventually at

258. SCJN, 6/5/70, *ED* 32-126.
259. Law 20,305 (*BO* 3/5/73).
260. CNCiv, Sala I, 30/3/95, *ED* 162-589.

the time that Article 132 NCCPC indicates because the Argentine judge that received the letter rogatory only provided procedural assistance to the foreign judge'.[261]

III. Treaties

573. The TMs of 1889 and 1940 contain relatively brief regulations on the area, something understandable if considering the time of drafting. At that time, international traffic had not reached the dynamic developed since the 1950s.

574. The scope of application was extended in the Treaty of Montevideo (TM) of 1940. While the TM of 1889 limited its scope to civil and commercial matters (Article 5), the TM of 1940 extended the scope to administrative litigation, criminal law, public documents, and documents executed by officers of a Member State (Articles 3, 5, and 11). Communications must be done through letters rogatory (Article 3 of both TMs).

575. Even when the TMs do not expressly establish which organism may request the assistance, the articles of the TMs implicitly reflect that the request must be done by judicial authorities (the latter derives from the texts of Article 9, TM of 1889 and Article 11, TM of 1940).

576. There are no express provisions regarding those authorized to deliver the letters rogatory. However, the TM of 1940 when stating the formal requirements does not include the legalization of signatures when the request is made through government diplomats. Accordingly, those officers may deliver a letter rogatory (Article 11).

577. Both TMs require legalization and authentication. The legalization is fulfilled when it complies with the laws of the place where the document is created. The authentication is fulfilled when performed by government diplomats located in the place where the letter rogatory is intended to be presented (Articles 3 and 4, of both TMs). As previously mentioned, the TM of 1940 does not require legalization of signatures in letters rogatory dealing with civil or criminal matters when delivered through government diplomats, or, if the latter are not available, by members of the consulate of the country that remits the letter rogatory (Article 11).

578. The TM of 1940 indicates that letters rogatory must be drafted in the official languages of the States that remit them. The letters must be translated into the official language of the State of destination. Such translations must be legalized (Article 11).

---

261. CNCom, Sala D, 13/9/90, *Federal Deposit Insurance Corporation v. Compania General Inmobiliaria, S.A., LL*, T. 1991-A-296.

579. Letters rogatory must be delivered according to the laws of the State of destination (Article 11, TM of 1889 and Article 13, TM of 1940). The denial to comply with letters rogatory has not been expressly provided in the TMs. Therefore, the reservation clause will be applied because it protects the principles that motivate the legislation of the State of destination. *OP* is included in the Additional Protocols of both TMs (Article 4).

580. Regarding financial costs that letters rogatory may generate, the TMs only indicate that parties interested in delivery of letters may appoint agents. The financial costs that the latter may generate will be paid by the parties interested in the delivery (Article 12, TM of 1889 and Article 15, TM of 1940).

581. The legislative gap regarding financial costs can be bridged by applying the principle of gratuitousness that is included in modern conventions on cooperation. It seems to be clear that costs must be paid by parties interested in the delivery of letters, yet those individuals that encounter costs have the right to collect them later according to the regime of costs of principal processes.

582. Argentina also subscribed other treaties on international judicial cooperation (see *supra* Part I Chapter 1). The following relevant documents can be mentioned: CIDIPs on Letters Rogatory and Additional Protocol; Inter-American Convention on Proof of and Information on Foreign Law; Convention on the Taking of Evidence Abroad in Civil or Commercial Matters and Additional Protocol; and Convention on Execution of Preventive Measures.

583. Letters rogatory can be delivered to the required organism by the interested parties, through judicial recourse by government diplomats or by the central authority that requires assistance or that returns the letters rogatory. The material scope of the convention is also settled, such as the requirements of execution.[262]

584. International judicial cooperation within MERCOSUR is contained in two documents that cross through the three degrees:

- Protocol on Judicial Cooperation and Assistance in Civil, Commercial, Labour, and Administrative Matters (Las Leñas, 1992)[263] and Complementary Agreement (1997).[264]
- Protocol on Precautionary Measures (Ouro Preto, 1994)[265] and Complementary Agreement (Montevideo, 1997).[266]

262. http://www.oas.org/juridico/english/treaties/b-36.html.
263. http://www.mercosur.org.uy/show?contentid=2602.
264. http://www.mercosur.org.uy/show?contentid=2921.
265. http://www.mercosur.org.uy/show?contentid=2620.
266. http://www.mercosur.org.uy/show?contentid=2921.

585. The delivery of letters rogatory is not limited to the judicial recourse. Central authorities, government diplomats, and interested parties, as in the case of the CIDIPs, are allowed to delivery letters rogatory.

§3. Compatibility of Different Sources

586. A convergence of diverse instruments takes place once the scope of elaboration of international judicial cooperation and the sources of provisions are analysed. Facing this scenario, and to favour a *cooperation value*, it was necessary to implement a harmonizing mechanism, that was achieved through the incorporation of specific clauses.

587. Several conventions have incorporated harmonizing clauses through which the text of the new provisions does not limit previous or future conventional provisions or does not limit the most favourable practices existing amongst States that are related in the subject matter.

Chapter 5. International Arbitration

588. Argentina subscribed the Convention on the Recognition and Enforcement of Foreign Arbitral Awards, New York, 1958. Local jurisprudence rendered numerous decisions according to the provisions of that convention.[267]

589. All Member States of MERCOSUR ratified the Agreement on International Commercial Arbitration of 1998.[268] Recent research indicates that no court decisions dealing with that agreement have been rendered.

590. Argentine domestic law includes provisions on commercial arbitration in the NCCPC (Articles 736–773) and in the different provincial procedural codes. Amongst the many provisions on domestic arbitration, are to be found those rules on object of claims, matters that exceed the scope of arbitration, capacity, form of agreements, contents, facultative clauses on appointment of arbitrators, and acceptance of appointments.[269]

---

267. CFedApel., Mar del Plata, 04/12/09, *Far Eastern Shipping Company v. Arhehpez S.A. s/ ejecución de laudo arbitral, ElDial,* 29/12/2009; Incom, Sala A, 31/10/2002, *Galapesca SA s. conc. Prev. s/ exequatur x Kerchrybprom*, www. csjn.gov.ar. Not applying it: Incom, 5/11/2002, *Reef Exploration Inc. v. Compañía General de Combustibles SA*, with comment by de M.B. Noodt Taquela, 'Comentarios de jurisprudencia sobre arbitraje', in *DeCITA* 1.2004 (Buenos Aires: Zavalía, 2004), 344.
268. In Argentina, Law 25,223, *BO* 2/1/2000.
269. *See* J.C. Rivera, *Arbitraje comercial internacional y doméstico* (Buenos Aires: Lexisnexis, 2007); F. Mastrangelo, 'Arbitraje. Juicio de amigables componedores. Algunas reflexiones en torno al control judicial del laudo arbitral. El soft law como técnica de complementación en el arbitraje internacional', *RDCO* 243, 203; R. Caivano, *Arbitraje,* 2ª ed. (Buenos Aires: Ad-hoc, 2008).

Table of Cases

A

A., M.S, SCJN, 26/3/2008, *DJ* 16/07/2008, *La Ley online*: AR/JUR/1693/2008: 415.

B

B., M. N. v. Agea S.A., CNCiv., Sala I, 11/11/2004, *La Ley online*: AR/JUR/4502/2004: 359.
Banco de Italia y Río de la Plata S.A. v. Banco Pan de Azúcar S.A. s/ diligencia preliminar, SCJN, 09/11/04, *LL* 17/06/2005, 7; *DJ* 26/05/2005, 303: 59.
Banco do Brasil S.A. v. Astilleros Corrientes S.A., Juz.Nac.Com., N° 7, Secretaría 14, 21/10/86, www.diprargentina.com: 415.
Behrens, Germán Federico o Hermann Friedrich s/ sucesión ab intestato, SCBA, 13/06/07, *La Ley online:* AR/JUR/10804/2007: 370, 444.
Bendelman, Ana s/ pedido de quiebra por Gutiérrez, Juan Alberto, CNCom., Sala A. 02/10/09, *La Ley Online*: AR/JUR/46140/2009: 336.
Benettar SAIC v. Benetton S.P.A., CNCom, Sala A, 30/5/91:456.
Berman, Evelina Geraldina Faustina, CNCiv., Sala C, 30/12/1957, JA 1958-IV-27: 172.
B., N. s. sucesión ab intestato, CNCiv., Sala I, 29/12/09: 60.
BII Creditanstalt International Bank Ltd. s/ pedido de quiebra promovido por Vizcaino Jose, CNCom., Sala D, 24/11/2010, *ElDial Express* 15/03/2010: 338.
Boo, Héctor José s. sucesión testamentaria, SCJN, 14/09/10, www.diprargentina.com: 151, 363.
Bratar S.A. v. Rocca, Bernardo E.,CNCom., Sala A, 20/08/2009, *JA*, 20/1/2010: 321.
Brunicardi, SCJN, (Fallos 319:2886): 137.

C

C., A.M. v. R., O.J., Juz. Civ. y Com., Pergamino, 02/02/2009,www.diprargentina.com: 149.
Cafes La Virginia S.A s/ apelación –por denegación de repetición, SCJN, 22/12/93, *ED,* 158-134: 25.

D

E

F

G

J

K

L

M

N

O

P

R

S

T

U

V

W

Z

Selected Bibliography

BOOKS

Albornoz, M. *Choice of Law in International Contracts in Latin American Legal Systems.* Mexico: Cide, 2009.

Alfonsín, Q. *Introducción a la Teoría del Derecho Internacional Privado.* Montevideo: Fundación Cultura Universitaria, 1946.

Alfonsín, Q. *Teoría del Derecho Privado Internacional.* Montevideo: Idea, 1982.

Alfonsín, Q. *Escritos Jurídicos.* Montevideo: Fundación Cultura Universitaria, 1975.

Alonso García, R. *Código de Derechos Fundamentales.* Madrid: Ed. Civitas, 2010.

Audit, B. *Droit international privé.* París: Economica, 1991.

Bartin, E. *Études de droit international privé.* París: 1889.

Bartin, E. *Principes de droit international privé selon la loi et la jurisprudence francaise.* París: 1920, 1932, 1935.

Belandro, S. *Derecho comercial internacional.* Montevideo: Asociación de escribanos del Uruguay, 2008.

Boggiano, A. *Curso de Derecho internacional privado. Derecho de las relaciones privadas internacionale*s, 5ta ed. Buenos Aires: Abeledo Perrot. 2006.

Boggiano, A. *International Standard Contracts: The Price of Fairness.* Dodrecht/Boston/London: Graham and Trotman/Martinus Nijhoff, 1991.

Boggiano, A. *Sociedades y grupos multinacionales.* Buenos Aires: Depalma, 1985.

Boggiano, A. *Derecho internacional privado*, 5ª edición, Buenos Aires: Abeledo Perrot, 2006.

Bossert, G. *Régimen jurídico del concubinato.* Buenos Aires: Ed. Astrea, 1997.

Busso & Petracchi. *Código civil anotado.* T. I. Buenos Aires: Ediar, 1945.

Caivano, R. *Arbitraje,* 2ª ed. Buenos Aires: Ad-hoc, 2008.

Calvo Caravaca, A.L. & J. Carrascosa González (eds). *Derecho internacional privado.* Vol. I y II. 10ª ed. Granada: Comares, 2009.

Carrascosa González, J. *Desarrollo judicial y derecho internacional privado.* Granada, Comares, 2004.

Chares Laver, R. 'The Legal System of Argentina', in *Modern Legal Systems Cyclopedia*, Vol. 10, edited by K.R. Redden. USA: William H. Hein & CO, 1994.

Ciuro Caldani, M A. *El Derecho internacional privado ante los procesos de integración.* Rosario: Fundación para las Investigaciones Jurídicas, 1998.

Clarkson, C.M.V. & J. Hill. *The Conflict of Laws.* 3rd ed. United States: Oxford, 2006.

D'Antonio, D.H. *Derecho de menores.* Buenos Aires: Ed. Astrea, 1994.

Selected Bibliography

Dicey, Morris & Collins. *The Conflict of Laws, in Fourth Cumulative Supplement to the Fourteenth Edition, in edited by Lord Collins of Mapesbury.* Great Britain: Sweet & Maxwell/Thomson Reuters, 2011.

Dreyzin de Klor, A. & D. Fernández Arroyo. *Derecho internacional privado argentino. Tratados en vigor y otros textos relevantes.* Buenos Aires: Zavalía, 2009.

Dreyzin de Klor, A. & T. Saracho Cornet. *Trámites judiciales internacionales.* Buenos Aires: Zavalia, 2005.

Dreyzin de Klor, A. *El Mercosur. Generador de una nueva fuente de derecho internacional privado.* Buenos Aires: Zavalía, 1997.

Dreyzin, A. & C.E. Echegaray de Maussion (eds). *Nuevos Paradigmas de Familia y su reflejo en el Derecho Internacional.* Córdoba: Ed. Advocatus, 2011.

Dreyzin de Klor, A. *Private International Law in Argentina*, The Netherlands: Kluwer Law International, 2011.

Dreyzin de Klor, A. *La aplicación del derecho extranjero. Contratos internacionales. relaciones de consumo.* Costa Rica: EJC. Serie monografías, 2015.

Dreyzin de Klor, A. (colaboración de Britos C.) *Tratado de Derecho de Familia según el Código Civil y Comercial de 2014*, Disposiciones de Derecho internacional privado,Tomo IV (Santa Fe: Rubinzal Culzoni, 2014).

Dreyzin de Klor, A. *Código Civil y Comercial de la Nación Comentado*, Tome XI, Articles 2666–2671. Modificaciones a las Leyes 17.801, 19.550 y 24.240, R.L. Lorenzetti, Director, Argentina: Rubinzal Culzoni Editores, 2015.

Feldstein de Cárdenas, S. *Contratos Internacionales. Contratos celebrados por ordenador. Autonomía de la voluntad. Lex Mercatoria.* Buenos Aires: Ed. Abeledo Perrot, 1995.

Feldstein de Cárdenas, S. 'Derecho internacional privado y de la integración', in *Colección de Análisis Jurisprudencial*, Buenos Aires: Ed. La Ley, 2007.

Fermé, L. *Tratado de derecho del trabajo.* Edited by A. Vázquez Vialard. Buenos Aires: Astrea, 1985.

Fernández Arroyo, D. (ed.). *Derecho internacional privado de los Estados del Mercosur.* Buenos Aires: Zavalía, 2003.

Fernández Rosas, J. & S. Sánchez Lorenzo. *Derecho internacional privado.* 5ª ed. Madrid: Thomson-Civitas, 2009.

Franca Filho, M.T., L. Lixinski & M.B. Olmos Giupponi. *The Law of Mercosur.* Oxford: Hart Publishing, 2010.

Fresnedo de Aguirre, C. *Curso de derecho internacional privado.* Tomo I y II. Montevideo: Fundación de Cultura Universitaria, 2013.

Gelli, M.A. *Constitución de la Nación Argentina comentada y concordada.* 2ª ed. Buenos Aires: La Ley, 2004.

Goldschmidt, W. *Derecho internacional privado.* 10 ed. updated by A. Perugini Zanetti. Buenos Aires: Abeledo Perrot, 2009.

Goldschmidt, W. *El S.O.S en el Derecho internacional privado.* Buenos Aires: Editorial de Belgrano, 1979.

González Campos, J. *Derecho internacional privado. Parte especial.* Madrid: Centro de Estudios Superiores, Sociales y Jurídicos Ramón Carande, 1993.

Haro, R. *La competencia federal. Doctrina, legislación y jurisprudencia.* Buenos Aires: Edit. Depalma, 1989.

Juenger, F.K. *Derecho internacional privado y justicia material*. México: Editorial Porrúa- Universidad Iberoamericana, 2006.
Kaller de Orchansky, B. *Nuevo Manual de Derecho Internacional Privado*. Buenos Aires: Plus Ultra, 1991.
Kleimanovich, J. *Código Procesal Civil y Comercial de la Nación comentado y anotado*. Tomo I. 4ta. ed. Ampliada y actualizada. Buenos Aires: Abeledo Perrot, 2009.
Kritzer, H. (ed.). *Legal Systems of the World. A Political, Social and Cultural Encyclopedia,* vol. I, A-D. USA: ABC-Clio, 2002.
Lloveras, N. & M. Salomón. *El derecho de familia desde la Constitución Nacional*. Buenos Aires: Universidad, 2009.
Lorenzetti, R.L. *Las normas fundamentales de derecho privado*. Santa Fe: Rubinzal- Culzoni, 1995.
Lorenzetti, R.L. *Teoría de la decisión judicial. Fundamentos de derecho*. Santa Fe: Rubinzal Culzoni, 2006.
Maekelt, T.B. *Teoría general del derecho internacional privado*. Caracas: Academia de Ciencias Políticas y Sociales, 2005.
Martínez Paz, F. *Introducción al Derecho*. Buenos Aires: Depalma, 1991.
Najurieta, M.S. *Coordinación de ordenamientos jurídicos en materia de adopción internacional*. Córdoba: Ediciones de la Academia Nacional de Derecho y Cs. Sociales de Córdoba, 2004.
Rubaja, N. *Derecho Internacional Privado de Familia. Perspectiva desde el ordenamiento jurídico argentino*. Buenos Aires: Abeledo Perrot, 2012.
Oyarzabal, M. *La nacionalidad argentina: Un estudio desde la perspectiva del derecho internacional público, del derecho internacional privado y del derecho interno argentino, con referencias al derecho de la integración*. Buenos Aires: La Ley, 2003.
Palacio de Caeiro, S. *Competencia federal civil-penal*. Buenos Aires: La Ley, 1999.
Parise, A. 'Legal Transplants and Codification: Exploring the North American Sources of the Civil Code of Argentina (1871)', in Gutiérrez Posse et al. *Informes de la Asociación Argentina de Derecho Comparado*. Buenos Aires: XVIII Congreso de la Academia Internacional de Derecho Comparado, 2010.
Pérez Royo, J. *Las fuentes del derecho*. Madrid: Tecnos, 1993.
Pereznieto Castro, L. *Arbitraje comercial internacional*. Méjico: Ed. Fontamara, 2006.
Pereznieto Castro, L.& Silva J.*Derecho internacional privado. Parte General*. 10° ed. México: Oxford University Press, 2015.
Ray, J.D., et al. 'Transport Law', in *International Encyclopaedia of Laws*, Supl. 22. The Hague: Kluwer Law International, 2007.
Rivera, J.C. *Arbitraje comercial internacional y doméstico*. Buenos Aires: Lexisnexis, 2007.
Samtleben, J. *Derecho Internacional Privado en América Latina, Teoría y práctica del Código Bustamante*. Vol. I. General Part. Translated from the original in German by C. Bueno-Guzmán. Buenos Aires: Depalma, 1983.
Samtleben, J. *Rechtspraxis und Rechtskultur in Brasilien und Lateinamerika*. Aachen: Shaker Verlag, 2010.

Scotti, L. *Código Civil y Comercial de la Nación analizado, comparado y concordado*, Tome 3, Articles 2666–2671, A.J. Bueres, Director (Argentina: Hammurabi Ed., 2015).
Shany, Y. *Regulating Jurisdictional Relations between National and International Courts*. New York: Oxford University Press Inc., 2009.
Silva, J.A. *Derecho internacional privado*. México: Ed. Porrúa, 1999.
Story, J. *Commentaries on the Conflict of Laws, Foreign and Domestic, in regard to Contracts, Rights, and Remedies*. Boston: Hilliard, Gray and Co., 1834.
Symeonides, S. 'United States of America' in *Private International Law*. Vol. 3 of International Encyclopedia of Laws. The Hague: Kluwer Law International, 2008.
Tagle de Ferreyra, G. (dir.). *Interés superior del niño. Visión jurisprudencial y aportes doctrinarios*. Córdoba: Nuevo Enfoque Jurídico, 2009.
Uzal, M.E. *Procesos de insolvencia en el Derecho internacional privado*. Buenos Aires: Ed. La Ley, 2008.
Van der Grinten, P. 'Abolishing Exequatur in the European Union: An Alternative', in *Crossing Borders Essays in European and Private International Law, Nationality Law and Islamic Law in Honour of Frans van der Velden*, edited by P. van der Grinten & T. Heukels. Deventer: Kluwer Law, 2006.
Vescovi, E. *Derecho procesal civil internacional*: *Uruguay, el Mercosur y América*. Montevideo: Idea, 2000.
Von Savigny F.C. *Sistema de Derecho Romano Actual*. Vol. VIII. 2ª ed. Madrid: Edición Góngora, 1879.
Von Savigny, F.C. *A Treatise on The Conflict of Laws and The Limits of their Operation in Respect of Place and Time*. Translated with notes by W. Guthrie. 2nd. ed. New Jersey: Rothman Reprints Inc., South Hackensack, 1972.
Weinberg, I. *Derecho internacional privado*, 2da. ed. Buenos Aires: Abeledo Perrot, 2004.
Wolf, M. *Private International Law*. 2da. ed. Oxford: 1950.
Woodman, G. *Interdisciplinary Studies of Comparative and Private International Law*, Vol. I, ed. Bea Verschraegen. Jan Sramek Verlag, 2010.
Zajtay, I. 'The Application of Foreign Law', in *Private International Law. International Encyclopedia of Comparative Law*, Vol. III.

ARTICLES

Bidart Campos, G. Comment of the case *Méndez Valles, Fernando v. Pescio A. M. s/ ejecución de alquileres*. CSJN, 26/12/95. LL 1996-C, 499–507.
Boele-Woelki, K. 'What Comparative Family Law Should Entail?', *Utrecht Law Review* 4(2) (2008).
Britos, C. 'De cara a la postmodernidad, la superación del conflicto de fuentes a la luz del camino de la coordinación'. *Suplemento de derecho internacional privado y de la integración*, *ElDial*, 26/11/2010.
Britos, C. 'Los Principios que iluminan el Derecho Internacional Privado en el Proyecto de Código Civil y Comercial', publicado en *La Ley* el 13/02/2014, Bs. As., Tomo 2014-A, ISSN 0024-1636.

Britos C. 'Una visión de los contratos internacionales electrónicos, desde el nuevo Código Civil y Comercial de la Nación', en *El Dial.com* el 3/12/2014, Citar: elDial DC1E25.

Britos, C. 'El certificado de idoneidad para adoptar en el extranjero: entre el rigor formal y la necesidad de velar por los derechos de la infancia', en*La Ley* – DJ 18/02/2015, 11. Cita Online: AR/DOC/4484/2014.

Britos, C. 'El rol de la constitucionalización en el derecho internacional privado actual, desde la mirada del nuevo Código Civil y Comercial, y el resplandor del control de convencionalidad', *La Ley* RCCyC 2015 (octubre), - RCCyC 2015 (diciembre), 16/12/2015, 245, Cita online: AR/DOC/3256/2015.

Caparelli, J.C. 'Las convenciones matrimoniales en el artículo 163 del Código Civil. Ley 23,515'. *La Ley* 1990-D, 659.

Dreyzin de Klor, A. Comment of the case *Compañía General de Negocios pide la quiebra Mihanovich, Ricardo L.*, CSJN, 24/02/2009, CNCom., Sala C, 27/04/10, in RDCO 237, 155/167, 'La CSJN ubica cada ficha en su casillero'. *DeCITA*, 11.2009, Insolvencia internacional.

Dreyzin de Klor, A. 'Comparecencia de un estado extranjero ante los tribunales argentinos'. Revista *La Ley*. Buenos Aires, 1995.

Dreyzin de Klor, A. 'Derecho aplicable al comercio electrónico', in N*ueva lex mercatoria y contratos internacionales*, edited by J. Oviedo Albán & A.L. Calvo Caravaca. Colombia: Ibañez, 2006.

Dreyzin de Klor, A. 'Los instrumentos de cooperación jurisdiccional del Mercosur ¿útiles a la asistencia?'. *RDPC* 2009-3.

Dreyzin de Klor, A. 'Una vez más, los niños como prenda de conflicto'. *Revista de Derecho de familia*, No 2011, II. Buenos Aires: Abeledo Perrot. 2011.

Dreyzin de Klor, A. 'Los principales desarrollos dentro del Derecho Internacional Privado en el próximo siglo en Argentina'. *Revista Mexicana de Derecho Internacional Privado,* Número Especial. México: D.F., 2000.

Dreyzin de Klor, A. 'Derechos Humanos, Derecho Internacional Privado y Activismo Judicial', en *XXXIX Curso de Derecho Internacional, Organización de los Estados Americanos*, Washington D.C., 2013; y en *El Dial.com*, elDial DC1A58.

Dreyzin de Klor, A. 'El alcance de la excepción convencional en materia de sustracción internacional de menores: un caso para tener en cuenta', in *Derecho de las Familias, infancia y adolescencia: una mirada crítica y contemporánea*, Graham M. & Herrera M. (Directoras), 1° ed., (Buenos Aires: Infojus, 2014).

Dreyzin de Klor, A. & Britos C. 'Una decisión judicial que preserva los principios tuitivos en orden a la restitución internacional de menores', 21/11/2014, MJ-DOC-6972-AR | MJD6972.

Dreyzin de Klor, A. & Ellerman I. 'La evolución de la responsabilidad civil extracontractual en el DIPr: a propósito de la sanción del nuevo Código Civil y Comercial de la Nación', *La Ley online:* AR/DOC/4036/2015.

Echegaray de Maussion, C. & M. Lucero. 'Transexualidad y sentencia extranjera de reasignación de sexo: Cuestiones de derecho sustancial y procesal'. *Actualidad Jurídica-Familia y Minoridad*, N° 60. Córdoba: Ed. Nuevo Enfoque Jurídico, April 2009.

Feldstein de Cárdenas, S. & M.S. Rodríguez. Comment of the case *Ulloa, Alberto s/ sucesión*, CSJN, 10/04/07, SJA 12/12/07.

Selected Bibliography

Garro, A. & M.P. Perales Viscasillas. 'Opiniones del CCIM-AC: Consejo Consultivo en materia de compraventa internacional de mercancías'. *DeCITA* 9, 2008, CEDEP.

Gerbaudo, G. 'Panorama sobre el régimen internaiocnl de los títulos valores en el Anteproyecto de Código Civil y Comercial de la Nación del año 2012', *Microjuris*, MJ-DOC-5788-AR, 15/5/2012.

Goicochea, I. 'Aspectos prácticos de la sustracción internacional de menores'. Jurisprudencia Argentina, 2006-I. *La Ley* 2006-C, 272.

Goicoechea, I. & Rubaja N. 'Procedimiento de restitución internacional de niños: pautas imprescindibles para la eficiencia del mecanismo convencional', *La Ley* 21/08/2015, Cita online: AR/DOC/2781/2015.

Goldschmidt, W. Comment of the case *Mandl, Federico A. M. s/ sucesión*, CNCiv., Sala C, 03/03/81, LL 1981-C,63.

Goldschmidt, W. 'Reforma del DIPr argentino'. *Revista Facultad de Derecho*, Universidad Nacional de Tucumán, No 12, 1955.

Grodecki, J.K 'Intertemporal Conflict of Laws'. *International Encyclopedia of Comparative Law* III, 1976.

Harrington, C. Comment of the case *Sanovo Internacional SA v. Ovoprot Internacional, s/ordinario*, CNCom., Sala F, 24/06/10, 'Responsabilidad por incumplimiento en la compraventa internacional de mercaderías'. *RDCO*, 2011.

Harrington, C. 'Transporte benévolo y seguro de responsabilidad civil del MERCOSUR: un caso para la reflexión'. *RDPC*, 2009-2. Santa Fe: Rubinzal Culzoni, 2009.

Hertz, M. 'La nueva Convención de UN sobre inmunidad de jurisdicción de los Estados y sus bienes, Su compatibilidad con el régimen argentino'. *ED* 215, 929.

Hooft, E.P. 'Las uniones de hecho (concubinatos) en el Mercosur y la necesidad de armonizar las legislaciones (y las jurisprudencias) de los Estados Parte'. Suplemento de Derecho internacional privado y de la integración. *El Dial*, November 2004.

Jayme, E. 'O Direito Internacional Privado e a Familia no Umbral do Seculo XXI', in *Cadernos do Programa de Pós-graduacao en Direito – PPGDIr./UFRGS*. Universidad Federal de Rio Grande do Sul. Vol. 1, N° 1, Porto Alegre, March 2010.

Kegel, G. 'Fundamental Approaches'. *International Encyclopedia of Comparative Law, Private International Law* 3.

Kemelmajer de Carlucci, A & E. Lamm. 'La persona transexual, menor de edad, competente para decidir sobre la intervención médica que requiere judicialmente'. *Semanario Jurídico* Nº 1637. Córdoba: T. 96, Nº 23.

Lagarde, P. 'Public Policy'. *International Encyclopedia of Comparative Law, Private International Law* III.

Lando, O. 'Private International Law, Contracts', in *International Encyclopedia of Comparative Law,* Vol III, edited by K. Lipstein.

Lima Marques, C. 'Confiança no comércio eletrônico e a proteção do consumidor (un estudo dos negócios jurídicos de consumo no comércio eletrônico)'. *Revista dos Tribunais*, Brazil, 2004.

Lipstein, K. 'Characterization'. *International Encyclopedia of Comparative Law* I.

Lucero de Godoy, M. & C. Echegaray de Maussión. 'La protección internacional del consumidor. Algunas propuestas para una codificación regional', in *Protección de los Consumidores en America*, trabajos de la CIDIP VII (OEA). Asunción: La Ley Paraguay S.A. Centro de Estudios de Derecho, Economía y Política –CEDEP-, 2008.

Lucero, M. & C. Echegaray de Maussion. 'Alimentos internacionales en el marco de la cooperación internacional'. *Actualidad Jurídica-Familia y Minoridad*, N° 68.

Mastrangelo, F. 'Arbitraje. Juicio de amigables componedores. Algunas reflexiones en torno al control judicial del laudo arbitral. El *soft law* como técnica de complementación en el arbitraje internacional'. *RDCO* 243, 203.

Menicocci, A. 'Reflexiones sobre el problema de las calificaciones en el Derecho Internacional Privado', in *El derecho privado ante la internacionalidad, la integración y la globalización – Homenaje al Profesor Miguel Angel Ciuro Caldani*, edited by A. Alterini & N.L. Nicolau. Buenos Aires: La Ley, 2005.

Menicocci, A. 'El régimen internacional jusprivatista sobre la capacidad de la persona humana en el Proyecto de Código Civil y Comercial de la Nación – Los problemas derivados del favor negotti', *ED* 5/3/2014, Buenos Aires.

Najurieta, M.S. 'El pluralismo metodológico en el Derecho Internacional Privado actual'. *ED,* Buenos Aires.

Noodt Taquela, M.B. Comment of the case *Reef Exploration Inc. v. Compañía General de Combustibles SA., Incom*, 5/11/2002, 'Comentarios de jurisprudencia sobre arbitraje'. *DeCITA* 1.2004. Buenos Aires: Zavalía, 2004.

Opertti, D. 'El problema de las sociedades comerciales extranacionales en el derecho internacional privado (en especial en la doctrina)', in *Temas de derecho internacional privado,* N° 4. Montevideo: FCU.

Padilla, M. Comment ot the case *Sejean, Juan B. v. Zacks de Sejean, Ana M.*, CSJN, 27/11/86. *La Ley* 1986-E, 648.

Radzyminski, A. 'La ley aplicable a las sucesiones en el derecho internacional privado argentino'. *ED* 143–746.

Ramayo, R.A. Comment of the case *Romero López, M. v. D'Auria*, CSJN, 10/10/2000. *ED* 192, 233–237.

Richard, E.H. 'Actividad ilícita de sociedad extranjera (indirect doing business) y su quiebra en el país (en torno a importantísimo fallo de la Corte)'. *ElDial Express*, 16/3/2009.

Rodríguez, M. 'Las Fuentes del Derecho Internacional Privado en el nuevo Código Civil y Comercial de la Nación', en *ElDial.com* 27/3/2015, elDial DC1EBE.

Rouillon, A. 'Cuestiones de derecho internacional privado en la ley concursal argentina 24,522', in *Anales de la Academia Nacional de Derecho y Cs. Sociales de Bs. As.*, 1999, year XLIV, N° 37.

Sagüés, N.P. 'Los tratados internacionales en la reforma constitucional argentina de 1994'. *LL*, 1994-E.

Sanchez Lorenzo, S. 'Estado democrático, postmodernismo y el derecho internacional privado'. *Revista de Estudios Jurídicos*, N° 10/2010. España: Universidad de Jaén, Segunda Epoca.

Selected Bibliography

Scotti, L.B. Comment of the case *D., O. A. v. C., T. M. s. cesación de cuota alimentaria*, CNCiv., Sala I, 31/08/04, *ElDial* 06/10/04, *Revista de Derecho de Familia N° 30* (March /April 2005).

Scotti, L., & Brodsky J. 'Los clásicos problemas del Derecho Internacional Privado relativos al Derecho Aplicable en el nuevo Código Civil y Comercial', in *En Letra* - año II, número 4 (2015), tomo I; https://enletra.files.wordpress.com/2015/09/el-4-i-scotti.pdf.

Usunier, L. 'Regulating the Jurisdiction of Courts in International Litigation: Towards a Global Answer in Civil and Commercial Matters', in *Yearbook of Private International Law*, Vol. IX, edited by A. Bonomi & P. Volken. European Law Publishers/Staempfli Publishers Ltd. Berne, 2007.

Uzal, M.E. 'La protección al consumidor en el derecho internacional privado'. *RDCO*, 1999.

Uzal, M.E., Comment of the case *Sabaté Sas S. A. en Covisan, P/conc.*, SCdeMza., Sala I, 28/4/2005. *LL* 2005-D, 247.

Uzal, M.E. 'Nuevo Código Civil y Comercial: la vigencia temporal, con especial referencia al Derecho Internacional Privado', *La Ley* RCCyC 2015 (julio), 01/07/2015, 50.

Weinberg, I., 'Sucesiones internacionales'. *La Ley* 1995-D-1204.

Vélez Sarsfield, D. *Civil Code of Argentina*, translated into English, with an Introduction and Index, trans. by Julio Romañach Jr., 2d ed., 2008.

Index

The numbers here refer to paragraph numbers.

Index